A Passion for Potatoes

"This is a cookbook that is fun to read . . . and lest you wonder just how far you can go with a potato, Marshall includes a . . . section on potato-based desserts."
—Karen Stabiner *L.A. Times*

"I own three copies of Lydie Marshall's *A Passion for Potatoes.* One sits in my kitchen, where I do the cooking; one waits at my desk, where I draw up the daily shopping list; and one lies by my bed, where I dream of the potato delights in store for tomorrow. . . . When I have finished cooking my way through *A Passion for Potatoes,* I will be amazed if nearly all of Lydie's potatoes have not become a part of my everyday routine."
—Jeffrey Steingarten, *Vogue*

"The ebulliently titled second book of New York cooking school director Marshall is aptly named. The humble and nutritious potato does deserve a volume of its own, and this one demonstrates the author's skill and sophisticated taste."
—Publishers Weekly

"Ms. Marshall's . . . verve and enthusiasm come through strongly in this celebration of spuds."
—Nancy Harmon Jenkins, *New York Times*

"Invaluable."
—Corby Kummer, *The Atlantic*

"Lydie Marshall, a cooking teacher in New York, has just come out with a cookbook, *A Passion for Potatoes,* that gives the potato its due."
—Trish Hall, *New York Times*

"An inviting new book."
—Florence Fabricant, *New York Times*

"From fritters to knishes to gnocchi, the offerings here, accompanied by authoritative observations in the margins, are often so appealing that I didn't mind being stuck in this little corner of cooking at all."
—Richard Flaste, *New York Times Book Review*

"Get yourself a copy of *A Passion for Potatoes.*"
—San Francisco Chronicle

"*A Passion for Potatoes* will make you want to take [Lydie Marshall's] courses—her recipe writing is clear and helpful, her variations on familiar themes are imaginative, and . . . each of these recipes reflects her own coherent and admirably unfussy taste."
—John Thorne and Matt Lewis, *Cookbook*

A Passion

LYDIE MARSHALL

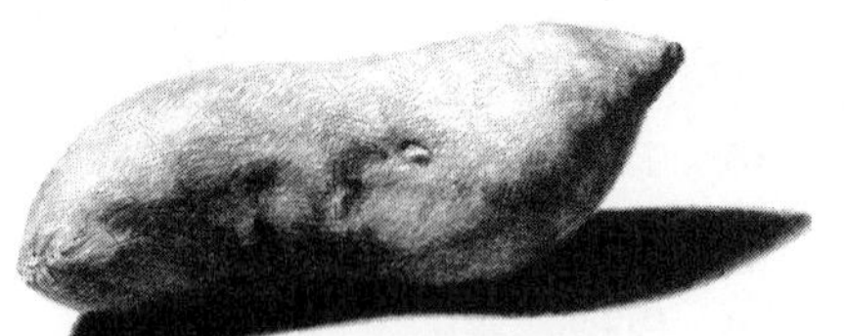

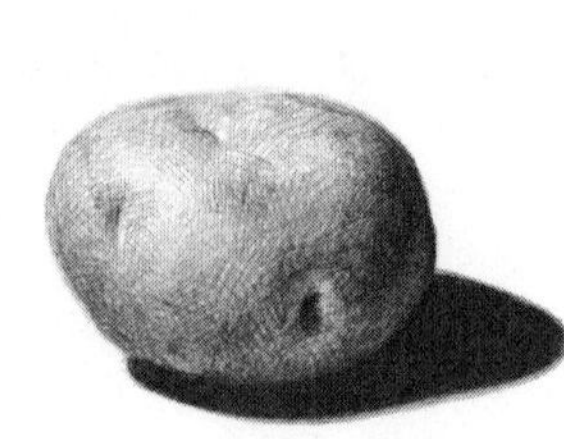

for Potatoes

FIRST EDITION

Designed by Helene Berinsky

Library of Congress Cataloging-in-Publication Data

Marshall, Lydie.
A passion for potatoes / Lydie Marshall.—1st ed.
p. cm.
Includes index.
ISBN 0-06-055323-5 (cloth)—ISBN 0-06-096910-5 (paper)
1. Cookery (Potatoes) I. Title.
TX803.P8M37 1992
641.6′521—dc20 91-50516

92 93 94 95 96 CG/RRD 10 9 8 7 6 5 4 3 2 1
92 93 94 95 96 CG/RRD 10 9 8 7 6 5 4 3 2 1 (pbk.)

To Charles Dunn ("Tonton")

My 91-year-old father, who has eaten potatoes all his life

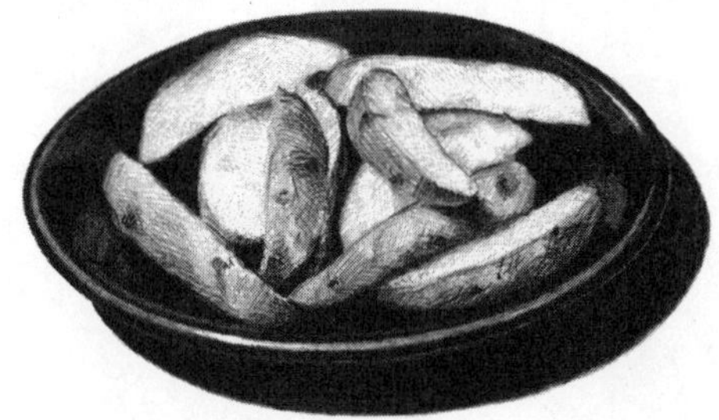

Contents

ACKNOWLEDGMENTS

I want to thank my family, friends, and students who have been eating potatoes every day, testing recipes with me for the past two years, and who still like potatoes.

In particular, I want to thank my editor, Susan Friedland, whose idea it was to write a book on potatoes.

FOREWORD

It doesn't surprise me that Lydie Marshall can make a lot of terrific dishes out of potatoes. In the first place, Lydie can make a lot of terrific dishes out of practically anything. If she did a rutabaga cookbook, I would vouch for it. I am confident that she could produce a stunning meal from the ingredients that were furnished to the cooks at my high school cafeteria—a meal whose main course would have no resemblance at all to what Lydie, when she first arrived at a Cleveland high school from France, might have called *viande grise.*

In the second place, I'm partial to potatoes. In restaurants where I remember the potatoes with particular fondness—restaurants ranging from Chez L'Ami Louis, in Paris, to Joe's Stone Crab, in Miami Beach—I have been known to say to the waiter, "Just bring us side orders of every kind of potato you can think of." My most recent foray into the world of competitive sports is as a co-organizer of a potato *latke* contest. One of my favorite articles of clothing is a T-shirt displaying the logo of Bud the Spud—a chip wagon that parks on Spring Garden Road, in Halifax, Nova Scotia, and dispenses the best french fries I've ever tasted.

During a time some years ago when fad diets seemed to be particularly popular, I even proposed an all-potato diet. It would permit all the potatoes the dieter could stuff down—french-fried, cottage-fried, home-fried, mashed, baked, shoestring, *latkes,* dumplings, au gratin, barbecue-flavored chips—as long as the dieter puts nothing else to his lips except 14 quarts of water a day.

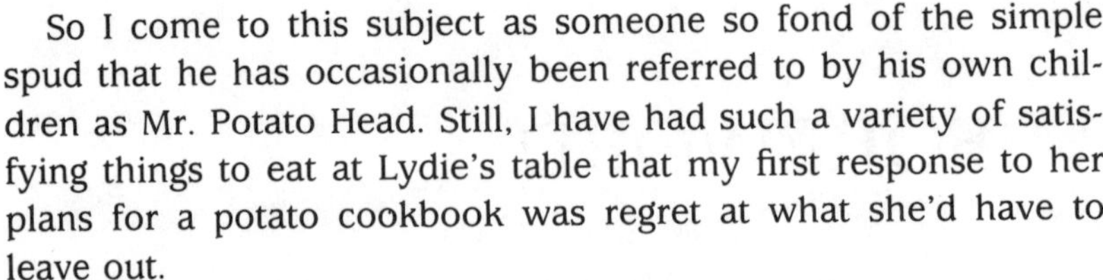

So I come to this subject as someone so fond of the simple spud that he has occasionally been referred to by his own children as Mr. Potato Head. Still, I have had such a variety of satisfying things to eat at Lydie's table that my first response to her plans for a potato cookbook was regret at what she'd have to leave out.

I thought particularly of *pistou*—a Provençal specialty that I once described as bearing the same resemblance to vegetable soup that a Greek wedding celebration bears to a bridge club tea. In the fall, when the cranberry beans begin to show up at the Union Square market, one of Lydie's principal New York hangouts, she sometimes invites us to her house for *pistou*, and I always leave confident that I can get through a long, cold winter.

When Lydie started working on this book, I said, "It's a shame your recipe for *pistou* won't be in there."

"But of course it will," Lydie said. "it has potatoes in it."

I hadn't particularly identified *pistou* with potatoes; I would have assumed it to be one of the lead recipes in a garlic cookbook. I realized that Lydie was interpreting potato recipes broadly—an approach that has my complete support. For all I know, she might have put in a rutabaga recipe that includes a potato or two. If so, try it.

—Calvin Trillin

INTRODUCTION

I have eaten potatoes practically every day for two years while doing research for this book, and I know now that I can eat potatoes forever. I never once tired of preparing and eating them. I believe that the potato is like a chameleon: It changes face and color with ease.

A potato is not just a potato, as some people tend to think. There are hundreds of varieties of potatoes, but we, the consumers, don't have much choice because American farmers mass-produce only a few varieties, such as the russet baking potato; the Superior, Kennebec, or Katahdin all-purpose potato; the Red La Soda, the Red La Rouge, the Red Pontiac, or the Red Nordland boiling potato (sometimes these red potatoes are called Red Bliss even though the real Red Bliss variety is not planted anymore). To complicate our lives, the potato wholesalers do not identify the potatoes by their varieties as they do in Europe, but mostly by where the potatoes were grown, so we see eastern, Long Island, Maine, or Idaho potatoes. Sometimes the potatoes are sorted by types (baking potatoes, all-purpose or boiling potatoes, new potatoes) and also by their color (red potatoes). It's all very confusing. What does it all mean? Now, there are places and there are potatoes. A place is not a potato. Different varieties of potatoes may be grown in the same places. and the same variety in different places.

It is the potato variety that determines its consistency, taste, and cooking characteristics. For example: The most famous

American potato is the Idaho potato called the Russet Burbank (see page xviii for its history). It's a baking potato, but within the russet potato family there are other russet varieties like the Russet Arcadia, another baking potato grown in places other than Idaho. "Potato scientists have speculated it was not the Russet Burbank that made Idaho famous, but rather Idaho that made the Russet Burbank famous."* Potatoes tend to grow better at a higher elevation than at sea level; they require long warm summer days and cool nights. Idaho produces quality potatoes because the soil is made of volcanic ash with a rich supply of trace minerals in it. However, the state of Washington also produces russets, the state of Maine produces russets, you can even find Long Island farmers growing russet potatoes.

Americans are very proud of their baked potato, and for very good reasons. There is nothing better than a perfectly baked potato, and every person I know has her own way of presenting a baked potato at the table. For an American, it's a sin not to eat the skin of a baked potato; for a European, the skin is what you throw out. Every time I made french fries for my husband, he would ask for thick peels so they could be fried, and once I served them to a bunch of French farmers who thought I had lost my mind! Today, I don't even bother to peel the potatoes for french fries.

Potatoes are also classified according to their starch content; high, medium, or low. High-starch potatoes like the russet, from Idaho, Maine, or wherever, are best baked, mashed, or deep-fried. They tend to crumble in the water when they are boiled and become soggy. I still boil them when I make bread or when I make mashed potatoes, but I watch them very carefully and as soon as they are tender, I quickly drain them.

The medium-starch potatoes, so-called "all-purpose potatoes," are exactly that; they also can be baked, fried, or mashed. They are moister than the russet potato and will hold better in boiling water. The choice between types is a matter of personal prefer-

**The Aristocrat in Burlap*, p. 26.

ence; some believe that a baked all-purpose potato needs less butter to moisten the flesh than does a russet baking potato.

Low-starch potatoes are firm-textured. They are sometimes referred to as "waxy" because of the somewhat shiny appearance of the flesh and its firm texture. Small Red La Soda, Red La Rouge and fingerlings, such as Lady Fingers and Ruby Crescents, or Creamers (any variety of firm-textured potatoes that are not bigger than 1-inch in diameter) are perfect for steaming, barbecuing, and roasting whole.

Harold McGee in *On Food and Cooking*, a scholarly book on the science and lore of the kitchen, mentions a simple test to perform which will determine if the potato is starchy (mealy) or waxy. Place potatoes in a brine of 1 part salt to 11 parts water; the waxy potatoes will float, while the starchy potatoes will sink. I tried the test mixing 1 cup kosher salt to 11 cups water in a mixing bowl. In that small amount of brine I tested ¼-inch slices of baking potato (russet), an all-purpose potato (Superior), and a small red potato (Red La Soda). At first the 3 slices of potatoes floated; slightly put out with the experiment I left them there, forgetting about the test. But 1 hour later I had results: The russet and Superior potatoes had sunk to the bottom and the Red La Soda was still floating.

A few years ago, Canadians created a new variety of potato, the Yukon Gold, a yellow flesh potato. The Yukon Gold is the darling of many chefs and potato aficionados. It's a potato of medium starch content; I use it as my all-purpose potato—for gratins, mashed potatoes, and fries. Small-sized Yukon Gold potatoes are treated like the boiling potatoes for steaming, roasting, or boiling whole. There are other yellow flesh potato varieties. Now available all year around in some supermarket chains, the yellow flesh potato is sometimes under the name of "gold" potato, "yellow" potato, or "yellow gold." Yellow flesh potatoes are prized in France, where the B15 (a medium-sized potato with dark yellow flesh), the Bintje (originally from Holland and widely used for french fries), the Desiree (a reddish-skinned potato with yellow flesh), and the Ratte (the most delicate potato, sometimes called "the quenelle of Lyon," shaped like a thick finger) are among the favorites of French cooks. Small independent farmers in the United States are now planting these European potatoes. I know someone in the East who had better luck growing the Desiree variety than the Yukon Gold variety, for example. It depends on the type of soil in the different locations.

There are four potato harvests in the United States. The fall harvest is the largest; 75 percent of the potatoes consumed in the United States are harvested during this period in northern states such as Maine and New York (Long Island). The winter harvest takes place in south Florida. The spring harvest comes from northern Florida, Arizona, and California. The summer harvest is from Virginia, California, Michigan, and Texas.

For an extensive list of potato varieties, consult the Ronnig-er's Seed Potato Catalogue (their address is Star Route, Moyie Springs, Idaho 83845), Seeds Blum (Idaho City Stage, Boise, Idaho 83706), or Johnny's Selected Seeds (Foss Hill Road, Albion, Maine 04910).

Refer to the consumer's guide on pages xxii–xxiii for a short selection of potato varieties that might help you make your choice.

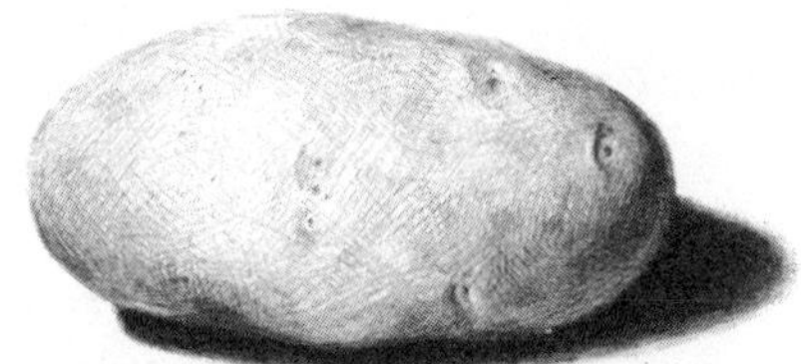

A Brief History of the Potato

Eons ago, potatoes grew wild in South America and were even found as far north as Colorado, but only the South American Indians knew what to do with them. As early as 750 B.C., potatoes were cultivated by the Andean Incas in Peru, Ecuador, and the northern part of Chile.

In the sixteenth century, the Spanish who had conquered the

Inca Empire are believed to have taken potatoes back with them to Spain. From there, the potato hopscotched throughout Europe. It appeared in Ireland and England around 1586, but not through the Spanish route.

For nearly 250 years, the English-speaking world believed that the potato reached the British isles via Virginia. This misunderstanding stems from John Gerard, a well-known botanist of his time, who wrote in his *Herbal* of 1596 that the potato came from Virginia. Apparently he thought this because his friend Thomas Hariot, just returned from Virginia with Sir Francis Drake, had given him some potatoes. What Gerard didn't know was that Drake had taken the potatoes on board in Cartagena, Colombia, when returning from South America. At any rate, Gerard gave some potatoes to Sir Walter Raleigh, who planted them on his property in Ireland. Another legend holds that perhaps the potato reached Ireland by accident. When the Spanish Armada was defeated, several ships foundered on the west coast of Ireland. These ships may well have had potatoes as part of the regular foodstuffs in the ships' pantries. Whether it came from the hands of Hariot or from the ruins of the Spanish Armada, the date of its entry to Ireland would still be about 1586–1587.

It took a long time for the potato to become accepted in Europe. Europeans mistrusted a vegetable that was not mentioned in the Bible, and because it was not grown from seed but rather from a tuber, it was said to be evil, responsible for many horrible diseases. It was the Irish, a good century later, in the late seventeenth century, who accepted the potato wholeheartedly and made it their most important crop.

In North America, the "Virginia potato" was planted around 1719, when Irish settlers came to Londonderry, New Hampshire. But like Europeans, Americans spurned potatoes. They used them for fodder and sold them to West Indian planters who wanted cheap food for their slaves. This attitude held until the second half of the nineteenth century, but then rapidly changed, perhaps because of the big Irish immigration at that time. Settlers came westward for different reasons, but it is the farmers who made their lasting impression on the new land. The Mormons, great farmers, planted potatoes on their farms around Salt Lake City but also in Idaho as they pushed outward seeking new lands. The discovery of gold in Idaho in 1860 helped widen the development of potatoes there, for gold miners ate potatoes and drank whiskey. In 1890, Idaho was admitted to the Union as the forty-third state. Idaho subsequently made the potato the most-eaten vegetable in the United States.

THE BIRTH OF THE RUSSET BURBANK

Luther Burbank created the Idaho potato without ever having lived in Idaho. In his New England garden, Early Rose (a potato plant) gave birth in 1872 to a seed ball (a fruit), which Burbank found on the vine of Early Rose after flowering. He decided to monitor day by day the pregnancy and birth of the fruit. Alas, one day it was gone, but Burbank knew that neither bird nor animal had eaten it so "day after day I returned and took up the search again and at last this patient search was rewarded. The missing seed ball was found." It gave birth to twenty-three seeds, and carefully he planted them all, one foot apart, and was rewarded with twenty-three potatoes. The star among them was sold to J. H. Gregory of Marblehead, Massachusetts, who named it Burbank. With the money he pocketed for his potato, Luther Burbank moved to California with ten tubers that Gregory had let him keep, which became the nucleus for the introduction of the Burbank potato to the West Coast. Luther Burbank never could reproduce another variety that was as good as his original Burbank potato.

How to Store Potatoes

Store-bought potatoes kept at room temperature are best used within 10 days of purchase. They will last longer if they are stored in a well-ventilated, dark room. The ideal storage temperature is between 45 and 50 degrees Fahrenheit (8 to 10 Celsius). Remove the potatoes from any plastic bags and store them loosely in a vegetable bin, or in a brown bag; otherwise they may rot and smell bad.

Don't refrigerate potatoes, because the starch converts into sugar. It will revert back to starch, though, if the potatoes are left at room temperature for several days.

Don't buy potatoes with a greenish tinge to their skins. This indicates that they have been badly stored. When they are exposed to light, they turn green, producing a toxic alkaloid called solanin. It is destroyed by cooking, but the potato flavor can turn bitter.

In the winter potatoes sprout easily. Cut out the sprouts before cooking the potatoes, because the sprouts are toxic, rich in alkaloids.

The Nutritional Value of Potatoes

The potato is a nutrient-dense food and is highly recommended in our daily diet. A 6-ounce potato yields 110 calories (the same amount of rice or pasta has 400 calories), 23 grams of carbohydrates, 3 grams of protein, no fat, no cholesterol. It has practically every vitamin except vitamin A. Jack Denton Scott in his article "Praise the Potato" states that "the U.S. Department of Agriculture reports that if a person's entire diet consisted of potatoes, he would get all of the riboflavin (B_2), one and a half times the iron, three to four times the thiamin (B_1) and niacin (B_3) and more than ten times the amount of vitamin C that the body needs."

But the nutritional value of the potato is altered by some meth-

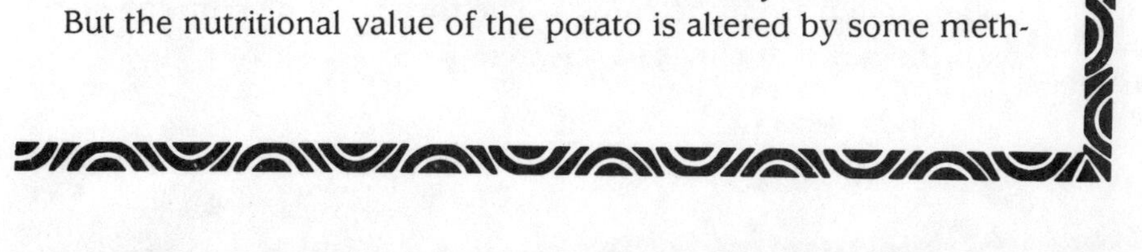

ods of preparation. Processing the potato will reduce its vitamin content. Keeping cooked potatoes for some hours and reheating them will do the same thing.

Potato Folklore

You can clean house with a potato or use it as a remedy.

To clean the inside of pots and pans: Boil potato peels in them.

To clean silver: Wash the silver with the water in which peeled potatoes have cooked.

But when I read that potatoes cleaned oil paintings, I had misgivings about trying it on one of my own. I asked my friend Denise Liote, an abstract painter, who said it was true indeed. When she picked her own paintings in my home to clean, I knew she was not kidding.

To clean an oil painting: First, dust the painting with a clean soft cloth. Choose a large potato, split it in half, and start rubbing the cut side of the potato on the canvas. Cut a slice off the potato when it gets dirty and continue doing so until you finish cleaning the canvas. Wet a soft clean towel and use it to brush off all the potato starch from the canvas. The towel will pick up the starch with the dirt that clings to it.

To clean window panes and mirrors: Cut a large potato in half and rub the cut side on the panes and mirrors. When the potato gets dirty, cut off a slice and continue. Rinse with clear water.

For tired eyes: Grate a potato and squeeze the liquid into a bowl. Soak compresses in the potato liquid and gently put them over your eyes for 15 minutes.

For intestinal parasites: Eat a potato salad seasoned with walnut oil every night for a week and you will get rid of them. Even if you don't, a potato salad every night won't hurt you.

A CONSUMER'S GUIDE TO SELECTED POTATO VARIETIES

Potato Name or Type	*Starch Content*	*Flesh*	*Shape*	*Color*	*Uses*
Russet Burbank, called "Idaho" potato but also grown in many other states	high	white	oval	brown	baking, frying, mashed, soups
Russet Arcadia, grown in Maine and other states	high	white	oval	brown	same as above
Eastern Potatoes all-purpose: Superior, Kennebec, Katahdin. Maine, Delaware, Long Island, Canada	medium	white	round	light tan	pancakes, pan frying, scalloped, gnocchi
Large Yukon Gold, Minnesota, Michigan, Canada, California	medium	yellow	round	light tan	roasted, salads, gratins, pancakes
Baby Yukon Gold, same as above	medium	yellow	round	light tan	steamed, roasted, barbecued
White Rose, also called Long White, grown in California and western states	medium-low	white	oval	light tan	scalloped, roasted, salads

Potato Name or Type	Starch Content	Flesh	Shape	Color	Uses
Small red potatoes, such as La Rouge or La Soda, grown in Florida	low	white	round	red	roasted, steamed, barbecued
Red Norland and Red Pontiac from midwestern states, Florida	medium-low	white	round	red	roasted, pan fried
Yellow Finnish, mostly grown in the West, Washington	medium-low	yellow	round	light tan	steamed, roasted, barbecued
Peruvian Blue, grown in several states by independent farmers	medium	blue	round	dark blue	roasted, mashed
Ruby Crescent and Fingerlings, grown by independent farmers	low	pale yellow	3″ long and 1″ wide	pink, light beige	steamed, roasted, barbecued

1. Appetizers

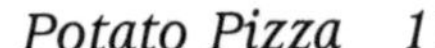

The russet baking potato has a starring role in this chapter; most of the recipes are made with baking potatoes, with the exception of the potato fritters, which are best made with a less starchy potato.

I put the potato pizzas and potato pies in this chapter, though they are also good as a main course for lunch or dinner.

Try this for summer picnics, informal buffets, lunch, cocktails, or as a filling for sandwiches. It's absolutely delicious and easy to make! The word terrine *applies to both the dish and its contents. The terrine is served in the dish, without unmolding. There are pretty porcelain, terra cotta, and enameled cast-iron terrines on the market, but it is not necessary to own one to make this dish—a glass loaf pan works fine.*

This terrine is looser in texture than a country pâté. It will be easier to scoop out the terrine with a spoon rather than trying to cut it in slices.

Terrine of Potatoes and Tuna

A 4-cup loaf pan or a terrine, oiled

2¼ pounds russet potatoes, peeled and diced into 1-inch cubes (6 cups)
1 cup hot milk
1½ teaspoons salt
Freshly ground pepper
1 red bell pepper
Two 6½-ounce cans tuna, packed in water
1 cup mayonnaise
1 tablespoon capers

GARNISH:
Gherkins and olives

In a saucepan, cover the potatoes with cold salted water and bring to a boil. Partially cover and cook for 15 minutes, or until tender. Drain and mash the potatoes with an old-fashioned masher, ricer, or through a strainer. Beat in the hot milk. Season with salt and pepper.

Char the red pepper over a burner. Put it in a plastic bag and set aside to cool. Peel and cut into ¼-inch cubes. Set aside.

Drain the tuna and process for 1 minute in the food processor.

Combine the mashed potatoes, tuna, and mayonnaise. Mix thoroughly. Fold in the red pepper. Taste and correct seasonings.

Put the mixture in the prepared mold and refrigerate until cold or overnight.

Decorate the top with capers. Serve with more capers, gherkins, and olives on the side.

Serves 10

Potato Madeleines

A 12-cup madeleine mold

1 pound russet potatoes, peeled and diced into 1-inch cubes (3 cups)
½ cup scalded milk
6 tablespoons (¾ stick) unsalted butter
1 egg
2 garlic cloves, peeled and mashed
1½ teaspoons salt
Freshly ground pepper
⅓ cup breadcrumbs, preferably homemade
1 cup sour cream
3 tablespoons minced chives

In a saucepan, cover the potatoes with cold salted water. Bring to a boil, partially cover, and cook for 15 minutes, or until tender.

Drain and mash the potatoes with a potato masher, ricer, or through a sieve.

Combine and mix the potatoes, hot milk, 2 tablespoons of the butter, egg, garlic, 1 teaspoon salt, and pepper.

Melt 2 tablespoons of the butter in a skillet and sauté the breadcrumbs until lightly golden.

Butter a 12-cup madeleine mold. Press about 2 teaspoons breadcrumbs in each cup. Freeze for 15 minutes.

Preheat the oven to 400 degrees.

Pack about 3 tablespoons of the potato mixture into each madeleine cup; melt the remaining butter and brush it over the madeleines. Place the mold on a baking sheet and bake until puffy and lightly browned, about 25 minutes.

Nudge each madeleine out of the pan with the point of a knife. Cool on a rack and serve with the sour cream mixed with chives and ½ teaspoon salt.

Makes 12 3-inch madeleines; serves 6

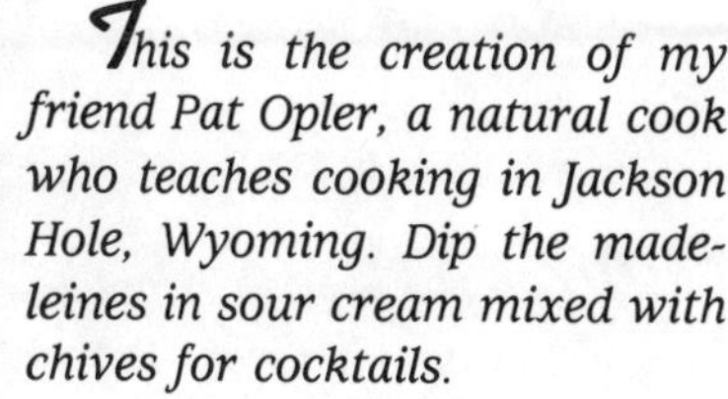

This is the creation of my friend Pat Opler, a natural cook who teaches cooking in Jackson Hole, Wyoming. Dip the madeleines in sour cream mixed with chives for cocktails.

La Mère Blanc's Mini Potato Pancakes with Minted Sour Cream and Salmon Caviar

If you are ever in the vicinity of Vonnas, a lovely French village near Lyon, don't miss lunch or dinner at Georges Blanc. It's a wonderful experience, though an expensive one. But never mind, for if there's one restaurant worth a splurge, this is it.

These minipancakes are the restaurant's signature. They are served as a side dish with the main course, though I like them to start a meal. To make them successfully, you should cook them in large nonstick skillets so they won't stick to the bottom of the pan and break. At the restaurant, they are made to order. At home, it is difficult to cook them at the last minute, but with two 10-inch nonstick skillets, you can make 4 to 6 at a time. If you are making the crêpes ahead of time, keep them on a cookie sheet and reheat in a preheated 300-degree oven for 5 minutes.

These pancakes also make a terrific dessert (page 226).

½ pound russet potatoes, peeled and diced into 1-inch cubes (1½ cups)
2 large eggs
2 egg whites
2 tablespoons flour or potato starch
½ cup milk
¼ cup heavy cream
½ teaspoon salt
3 tablespoons unsalted butter

FOR THE SOUR CREAM AND MINT TOPPING:

1 cup sour cream
2 tablespoons minced fresh mint
½ teaspoon salt
½ teaspoon lemon juice

8 ounces salmon caviar

In a saucepan, cover the potatoes with a large amount of cold salted water. Bring to a boil, partially cover, and cook for 15 minutes or until tender. Drain and mash the potatoes with a potato masher, ricer, or through a strainer.

Beat in the eggs 1 at a time, the egg whites, flour, milk, and cream. Season with salt. Set aside for at least ½ hour, but do not refrigerate.

To clarify the butter, melt it slowly and skim off the white foam on top. Scoop out the clear liquid and discard the milky residue at the bottom of the pan.

Combine the sour cream, fresh mint, salt, and lemon juice. Refrigerate until ready to serve.

Brush clarified butter in 1 or 2 large nonstick skillet(s). Heat pans over medium heat and when their bottoms are too hot to touch, drop 2 tablespoons (⅛ cup) of the batter in a pan. It will spread into a 4-inch circle. You should be able to make 2 to 3 crêpes at a time. Cook for 1 minute, then with a pancake turner gently nudge each crêpe all around its sides and shake the skillet(s) to loosen the crêpes. When they are lightly golden on the bottom, flip over and cook 1 to 2 minutes more. Repeat until all the batter is used.

Spread the sour cream mixture on the crêpes and decorate each with a dollop of caviar.

Serves 6 to 8 (3 cups of batter make 24 4-inch crêpes)

Crêpes Marcel

At Chez Marcel, a bistro in my Paris neighborhood, Marcel served delicious crunchy crêpes lightly stuffed with mashed potatoes, then deep fried. I always ate one crêpe to begin the meal there, but they are just as good for lunch with a salad. The mashed potato filling changed often at Marcel's, depending on what leftovers he mixed in. Marcel was thrifty, and retired to the Riviera at a relatively young age.

- **2 cups batter for Frances's Blintzes (page 224), omitting the vanilla extract, or your favorite crêpe batter**
- **½ cup mashed potato stuffing for knishes (see page 8), or Mashed Potatoes with Scallions (page 109)**
- **½ cup corn oil**

Prepare the blintzes or crêpes. Spread a thin layer of mashed potato on each blintz or crêpe and fold in quarters; flatten each crêpe with the palm of your hand. It can be prepared to this point several hours before serving.

In a large skillet, heat the oil to 325 degrees. Add 3 or 4 blintzes or crêpes at a time, depending on the size of the skillet. Fry until crispy on 1 side, turn and fry on the second side. Drain on paper towels. Repeat with the second batch. Serve immediately.

Makes 8 10-inch crêpes, serving 8 as an appetizer, 4 as a main course

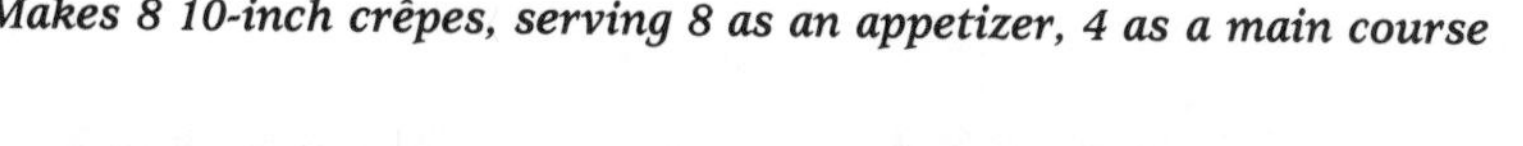

Esther Strauss, one of my students, was inspired to make these wonderful puff pastry potato goodies during the year of my potato research. They are well worth the work if you enjoy making puff pastry, but you can buy commercial puff pastry sheets, which will cut down drastically on the preparation time.

Puff Pastry Knishes

½ pound russet potatoes, peeled and diced into 1-inch cubes (1½ cups)
1 cup thinly sliced scallions
Salt
Freshly ground pepper
½ pound puff pastry dough, homemade or commercial

In a pan, cover the potatoes with cold salted water. Bring to a boil, partially cover, and cook for 15 minutes, or until tender.

Drain and mash the potatoes with a potato masher, ricer, or through a strainer. You should have 2 cups of loosely packed mashed potatoes.

Combine the potatoes and scallions; season with salt and pepper. Set aside to cool.

Dust a work surface with flour and cut the puff pastry in half. Refrigerate one half while you roll the other into a 12-inch by 18-inch rectangle. Transfer to a cookie sheet and refrigerate for half hour to firm up the dough.

Cut six 3- by 2½-inch rectangles from each piece of dough and once more refrigerate, placing wax paper between each layer.

For each knish, mound 2 tablespoons of well-packed potato mixture in the upper half of the rectangle. Lightly brush water on the outer ⅛ inch of the pastry. Fold the pastry over the potato stuffing and seal the edges, pushing down with the back of a fork.

Put the knishes on a cookie sheet lined with parchment paper and refrigerate until ready to bake. They can be prepared several hours ahead.

Preheat the oven to 350 degrees.

Bake the knishes in the preheated oven for 30 minutes, turning them over once. They should be golden brown. Serve warm.

Makes 12 individual knishes about 3 by 2½ inches

Knishes in Phyllo Dough

16 phyllo leaves
½ pound (2 sticks) butter, melted
2 cups mashed potatoes with scallions (page 8)

Roll out 1 phyllo sheet at a time, using a damp towel to cover the others to prevent them from drying out. Work fast; a phyllo leaf dries out quickly and cracks easily.

Each phyllo leaf will yield two 2- by 3-inch knishes.

Lightly brush 1 phyllo leaf with melted butter and fold it in quarters, lightly brushing with butter after each fold. Fold again in quarters, brushing with butter after you fold. (You will need about 1 tablespoon melted butter for each leaf.)

Cut the folded leaf in half; mound 1 tablespoon mashed potatoes near one end, butter the edges, and fold the other end over the filling, pinching the edges to seal.

Preheat the oven to 350 degrees.

Bake for 20 minutes, turning once. Serve warm with drinks.

Makes 32 2- by 3-inch knishes

Potato Fritters

For these fritters, I combined two classic French recipes, pommes dauphine (mashed potatoes and cream puff dough) and beignets pignatelli (cream puff dough mixed with pignoli nuts and smoked ham). These fritters are best with drinks.

1 pound Yukon Gold, Superior, or White Rose potatoes, peeled and diced into 1-inch cubes (3 cups)
½ cup pignoli nuts
3 tablespoons unsalted butter, softened
½ cup diced cured ham
1 teaspoon salt
Freshly ground pepper
Pâte à Choux (Cream Puff Dough) (page 11)
1 quart corn oil for deep-frying

Preheat the oven to 300 degrees.

In a saucepan, cover the potatoes with cold salted water and bring to a boil. Partially cover and cook for 15 minutes, or until tender.

Roast the pignoli nuts on a cookie sheet for 10 minutes.

Drain and mash the potatoes with a potato masher, ricer, or through a strainer, 1 potato at a time. You should have 3 cups. Over medium heat, beat in the butter. Fold in the nuts and diced ham. Season with salt and pepper.

Combine and mix the cream puff dough and the mashed potatoes.

(The recipe can be prepared to this point several hours before dinner. I sometimes make the batter the day before frying and keep it refrigerated.)

Deep-fry the fritters just before serving: Fill a deep-fryer, a wok, or a deep pan with corn oil to about one-third of its capacity. Heat the oil to 300 degrees on a deep-fry thermometer. Dip a spoon in hot water, shake the water off, and shape a fritter the size of a

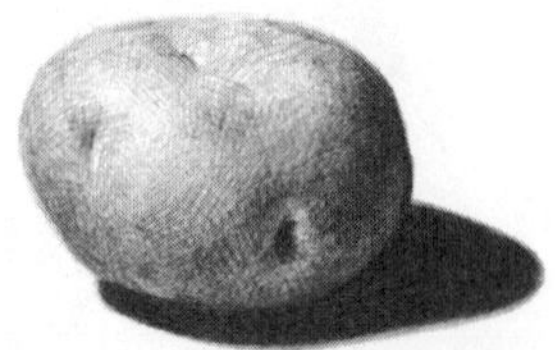

big olive. Fry about 10 fritters at a time. Turn them in the oil and fry until the fritters start bursting open, making them look like little pregnant puffs.

With a slotted spoon, drain and transfer the fritters to a platter, and continue deep-frying the remaining fritters. Sprinkle with salt and serve.

Makes about 30 fritters; serves 8 to 10

Pâte à Choux

CREAM PUFF DOUGH

- **1 cup plus 2 tablespoons water**
- **½ teaspoon salt**
- **7 tablespoons unsalted butter, cut into 1-tablespoon pieces**
- **1 cup plus 1½ tablespoons all-purpose flour**
- **1 cup eggs (4 large)**

In a heavy-bottomed saucepan, combine the water, salt, and butter and bring to a boil. As soon as the water boils and the butter is melted, quickly turn off the heat and add the flour all at once. Start beating vigorously, combining flour, water, and butter with a wooden spatula. Turn on the heat again and, still stirring, reheat the dough for 30 seconds. Turn off the heat.

Working quickly, beat in ¼ cup egg at a time, using a wooden spatula, or beat the dough in a heavy-duty mixer. Beat until the dough is smooth before adding the next ¼ cup egg.

Combine the dough with mashed potatoes for Potato Fritters (page 10) or French Gnocchi (page 191).

Makes 2¾ cups pâte à choux dough

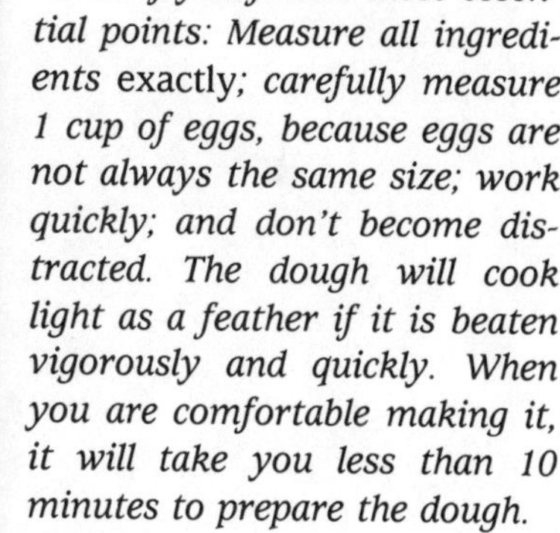

It's a cinch to make pâte à choux if you follow these essential points: Measure all ingredients exactly*; carefully measure 1 cup of eggs, because eggs are not always the same size; work quickly; and don't become distracted. The dough will cook light as a feather if it is beaten vigorously and quickly. When you are comfortable making it, it will take you less than 10 minutes to prepare the dough.*

Potato Pie in Phyllo Pastry with Bacon and Fresh Thyme

One 11-inch tart pan with removable bottom

½ pound slab bacon or pancetta, in 1 piece
2 pounds russet potatoes, peeled and sliced 1/16 inch thick (6 cups)
1 large onion, peeled and thinly sliced
2 tablespoons fresh thyme leaves
1½ teaspoons salt
Freshly ground pepper
½ cup heavy cream
8 phyllo leaves
3 tablespoons unsalted butter or margarine, melted, for the phyllo leaves

Cut the bacon or pancetta into strips, ¼ inch wide and ½ inch long. In a large skillet, sauté the strips until crisp. Drain on paper towels.

In a large bowl, combine the potatoes, onion, thyme, salt, pepper, cream, and bacon. Toss with your hands, thoroughly mixing all the ingredients. Set aside.

Unroll the phyllo leaves on a table and, working quickly, lightly brush butter on 1 leaf, fold it in half lengthwise, and brush butter on both sides of the folded leaf.

Place 1 end of the folded leaf in the center of the tart pan while the other end overhangs the side of the pan. Repeat with 7 more leaves, brushing with butter, folding, buttering, and overlapping them in the center of the pan, but barely touching at the outer edge, to create the spokes of a wheel.

Fill the prepared tart pan with the potato mixture; if there is any cream left over in the bowl, pour it over the potatoes.

Lift the end of the last pastry leaf placed in the pan and drape over the potatoes, twisting the leaf at the center of the pie. Continue with the remaining leaves, entirely covering the potatoes.

The center will have decorative twists. Lightly brush with butter.

Preheat the oven to 350 degrees.

Bake the pie in the center of the oven for 1 hour and 30 minutes; loosely cover with aluminum foil if the top browns too fast.

Serves 6

Potato Pie with Red and Yellow Peppers

In this lighter version of potato pie, I replace the bacon with colorful peppers.

- 2 pounds russet potatoes, peeled and sliced 1/16 inch thick (6 cups)
- 1 large onion, peeled and thinly sliced
- 1/4 cup olive oil
- 1/4 cup minced fresh basil
- 2 teaspoons salt
- Freshly ground pepper
- 1 large red pepper
- 1 large yellow pepper
- 8 phyllo pastry leaves

Toss the potatoes, onion, oil, basil, salt, and freshly ground pepper together. Set aside.

Meanwhile, char the peppers over a burner. Put them in a plastic bag and set aside to cool. Peel the peppers, remove the stems, seeds and membranes, and cut the flesh into 1-inch strips.

Follow the instructions in the preceding recipe for lining the tart pan with phyllo dough.

Put half the potato mixture in the tart pan lined with the phyllo pastry leaves. Arrange the pepper strips evenly over the potatoes and layer the remaining potatoes on top. Cover the pie with the phyllo leaves and bake following the instructions in the preceding recipe.

Serves 10 as an appetizer, or 6 for lunch or supper

Potato and Apple Tart with Sautéed Chicken Livers

This tart is best eaten hot. I serve it as an appetizer. Without the chicken livers, it's a good dessert (see the variation following this recipe).

The potato and apple slices should be the same size to create a lovely concentric pattern.

An 11-inch tart pan with removable bottom

4 ounces puff pastry dough, commercial or homemade
1 1/4-pounds Yukon Gold, Red Nordland, White Rose, or russet potato, peeled and sliced 1/16 inch thick (3/4 cup)
3/4 cup 1/16-inch-thick slices peeled, cored, and quartered golden apples
Salt and freshly ground pepper
4 tablespoons unsalted butter
1/2 cup chicken livers
1 tablespoon wine vinegar

Dust flour on a working surface and roll out the dough to 1/16 inch thick. Line the bottom and sides of the tart pan with the pastry. Trim the edges and reserve the extra dough for knishes (see page 8). Prick the bottom of the dough. Freeze until ready to use (it can stay frozen several weeks).

Stack the potato slices and cut them in half lengthwise. The potato and apple slices should be the same shape and size.

Fill the prepared tart pan with potato and apple slices, overlapping them in a concentric pattern in one layer only. Don't fill the center of the pastry; leave a 1-inch circle uncovered.

Gently fold the edges of the pastry over the potato and apple slices; only 1/2 inch or so of the filling will be covered.

Preheat the oven to 400 degrees.

Sprinkle 1/2 teaspoon salt and grind fresh pepper over the potatoes and apples. Dot the surface with 2 tablespoons butter shavings.

Bake the tart for 25 minutes.

Five minutes before the tart comes out of the oven, melt 2

tablespoons butter and sauté the whole chicken livers for 3 minutes. Deglaze the pan with the vinegar, boiling it down until it coats the livers. Slice the livers.

Decorate the center of the tart with the livers and serve immediately.

Serves 8 as an appetizer; 4 for lunch

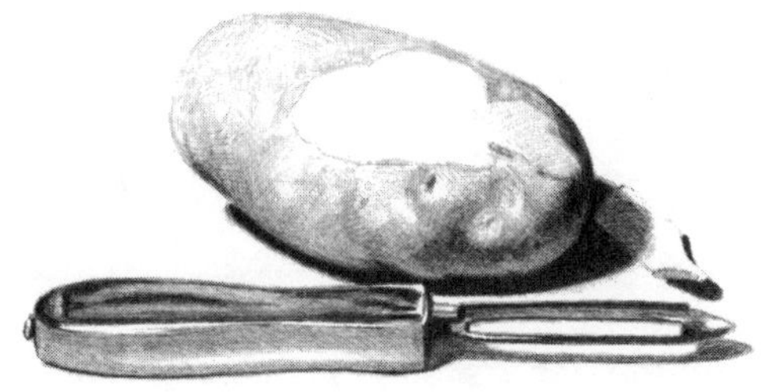

Potato and Apple Tart for Dessert

2 tablespoons melted apple jelly
1 tablespoon sugar

Prepare the tart according to the preceding recipe, filling the tart with potato and apple slices, dotting with butter shavings but omitting salt and pepper. Brush apple jelly over the pastry edges and potato and apple slices. Bake for 25 minutes. Sprinkle with sugar and serve hot.

Roquefort and Potato Tart

½ pound tomatoes
1½ teaspoons salt
1 tablespoon mustard
1 egg, lightly beaten
One 11-inch unbaked tart shell (recipe follows)
½ cup crumbled Roquefort cheese
½ pound russet potatoes, peeled and sliced ⅛ inch thick (1½ cups)
1 medium onion, peeled and sliced ⅛ inch thick (⅔ cup)
Freshly ground pepper
1 tablespoon minced fresh basil
2 tablespoons olive oil

Preheat the oven to 425 degrees.

Quarter the tomatoes and scoop out all the inside pulp (save for a sauce or stock). Dice the tomato shell into ¼-inch cubes and transfer to a strainer placed over a bowl. Sprinkle with 1 teaspoon salt.

Mix the mustard and egg together and spread it in the bottom of the unbaked tart shell. Sprinkle the Roquefort over it.

Overlap the potato and onion slices on top of the cheese. Sprinkle ½ teaspoon salt and freshly ground pepper over the potatoes and onions.

Combine the tomatoes with the basil and olive oil. Sprinkle the tomato mixture over the potatoes and onions.

Bake in the middle of the oven for 30 minutes. Serve hot.

Serves 8 for an appetizer, 4 for lunch

Potato Pizza

A 12- by 17-inch jelly roll pan, or two 11-inch tart pans with removable bottoms or pizza pans

- 10 ounces (1 cup) dough for Eliza Acton's Potato Bread (page 60)
- 10 ounces fresh unsalted mozzarella, coarsely grated on a hand grater (2 1/4 cups)
- 2 large garlic cloves, peeled and minced
- 3 tablespoons olive oil
- 1 1/2 teaspoons salt
- 1/2 pound Yukon Gold, Red Nordland, White Rose, or russet potatoes, peeled and sliced 1/16 inch thick (1 1/2 cups)
- 1 tablespoon minced fresh rosemary

Roll out the bread dough and place in the jelly roll pan, or cut the dough into 2 pieces and roll them to fit the two tart or pizza pans.

Combine the mozzarella, garlic, 2 tablespoons olive oil, and 1 teaspoon salt. Spread the mixture over the dough.

Put the potato slices in a large bowl of cold water as you slice them. Drain and pat dry. Overlap the potatoes very slightly over the cheese.

Brush on the remaining 1 tablespoon olive oil and sprinkle the rosemary and the remaining 1/2 teaspoon salt over the potatoes. Let stand 30 minutes or so in a warm place.

Preheat the oven to 425 degrees.

Bake in the middle of the oven for 30 to 35 minutes, or until the potatoes are golden brown around the edges.

Serve with drinks or for lunch with a tossed green salad.

Makes a large pizza serving 10 with drinks; 6 as a main course

Mom and Pop stores are still alive and well. Joe's Dairy Store on Sullivan Street in New York City, where I buy fresh mozzarella, closes for lunch every day! The store is minuscule, the kitchen even smaller, partitioned off behind the store; it has a small apartment stove on which mom or pop makes the best mozzarella in New York City. When I make pizza, I go to Joe's for today's mozzarella.

When making pastry dough in the food processor, do not process the flour, butter, and water until it becomes a ball; stop when the mixture looks like coarse cornmeal. Pinch a small amount of dough between your fingers, checking to see if the mixture sticks together. The rolled out dough keeps in the freezer for several weeks and can be baked frozen. It's great to have a reserve of unbaked tart shells in the freezer when the unexpected guest is on your front step.

French Pastry Dough

8 tablespoons (1 stick) unsalted butter
1 cup flour
A pinch of salt
2 to 3 tablespoons cold water, depending on the weather

Cut the butter into teaspoons and freeze for 30 minutes.

Put flour, salt, and butter in the bowl of a food processor fitted with the steel blade. Process for 10 seconds, then add 2 tablespoons water in humid weather or 3 tablespoons in dry weather. Process for another 10 seconds.

Dump the mixture on a table or counter and bind a small amount at a time with the heel of your hand, using a sliding motion to incorporate the butter and flour smoothly.

Gather the dough into a ball and flatten it. Wrap in wax paper and refrigerate for 15 minutes, just enough time to firm up the butter.

Flour the pastry surface and rolling pin and roll out the dough to a 13-inch circle; line an 11-inch tart pan with a removable bottom with the dough, trimming the excess. Prick the bottom. Refrigerate for 2 hours or freeze until ready to bake.

Makes 10 ounces of pastry dough

Bucheron Croque Monsieur

One 12-inch-long loaf Eliza Acton's Potato Bread (page 60), cut into 1/4-inch-thick slices
8 1/2 ounces goat cheese (Bucheron)
3 tablespoons plain yogurt
1 garlic clove, peeled and chopped
Pinch salt

Preheat the oven to 300 degrees.

Arrange the slices of bread on cookie sheets and toast on 1 side. Cut each slice of bread on the diagonal.

Process the cheese with the yogurt, garlic, and salt until smooth.

Turn the broiler on high.

Spread the cheese mixture on the bread. Broil 4 inches from the broiler element for less than 1 minute, or until the cheese starts melting. Serve with drinks.

Serves 12

2. Soups

The potato plays its most important, largely unsung, role in soups. It binds, it enriches, it thickens; in all, it helps create the best soups. I use such starchy potatoes as the Russet Burbank (Idaho baking) potato for body when I purée a soup. I use all-purpose potatoes like Yukon Gold, Red Pontiac, White Rose, or the large Red Nordland when the vegetables are not puréed in the soup.

For most of my family soups, I cook chicken or turkey parts with the vegetables instead of making chicken broth; it cuts down on time and work. Supermarket butchers cut up so many chickens and turkeys to package that there are plenty of leftover carcasses, which are packaged and sold at a fraction of the price of the meat. I seek them out and freeze them neatly packed in 1- to 2-pound portions, ready to put in a soup whenever I make one—practically every day in the winter.

Soups made with water only can still be tasty. Put 1 tablespoon butter or margarine in the bottom of individual bowls and pour the hot soup over it.

Always serve your soups boiling hot.

On cold afternoons, I substitute potato soup for my usual cup of tea. This comforting soup soothes the spirit. It is best drunk as soon as it is made. Left in the refrigerator, it thickens into a heavier soup; it's still good but its appeal changes.

Light Potato Soup

- **½ pound russet potatoes, peeled and diced into 1-inch cubes (1½ cups)**
- **1 tender celery branch with leaves, diced (½ cup)**
- **1 pound chicken or turkey backs, cut up in small pieces**
- **1 small onion, peeled and diced (½ cup)**
- **1 tablespoon salt**

Combine all the ingredients with 5 cups water in a stockpot. Bring to a boil, cover, and simmer over medium heat for 1 hour.

Strain into a bowl. Pick through the solids to remove all the chicken pieces (discard the bones and keep the meat for sandwiches). Process the vegetables until smooth, gradually adding the liquid.

Reheat until almost boiling. Pour into cups and drink.

Makes 5 cups of broth

The Concierge's Potato Soup

- 1 ½ pounds russet potatoes, peeled and diced into 1-inch cubes (4 cups)
- 1 pound carrots, peeled and cut into ½-inch slices (2 cups)
- 2 medium-sized onions, peeled and diced (2 cups)
- 1 garlic clove, peeled
- 2 pounds chicken or turkey backs, cut up
- 1 ½ tablespoons salt
- 1 teaspoon freshly ground black pepper
- 8 tablespoons margarine (optional)
- Parsley (optional)

In a stockpot, cover the vegetables and chicken bones with 8 cups cold salted water and bring to a boil. Cover the pot and simmer over medium heat for 1 ½ hours.

Discard the bones (pick the meat off the bones and add it later to the soup, or keep it for sandwiches). Purée the solids in a food processor or a vegetable mill, gradually adding the broth.

Reheat the soup. Season with freshly ground pepper and more salt if necessary. Serve very hot.

Optional: If the soup was made without chicken bones, put 1 tablespoon margarine into each of 8 soup bowls. Ladle in the hot soup and garnish with parsley.

Serves 8

In Paris, in the forties and fifties, I knew this soup as Le Potage de la Concierge, the janitor's soup. When you entered an apartment building in the evening, you were greeted by kitchen aromas coming from the concierge's living quarters, and by the concierge herself, who always checked on the comings and goings of her tenants and their guests. The soup was vegetarian; a pat of margarine (butter was hard to get during World War II) was put in individual plates just before the steaming soup was poured over it.

I have a Portuguese friend whose name fits him perfectly, John da Graça de Deus (John of the Grace of God). He is a marvelous craftsman who builds and renovates buildings with flair and gusto, for whom nothing is impossible. He happens to be a natural cook too, so when he speaks I listen. This chowder comes from his village. It can be served as a main meal by poaching a cod steak in it if you wish.

Portuguese Chowder

1 dozen cherrystone clams
6 oysters (not shucked)
⅓ cup olive oil
2 garlic cloves
1 bay leaf
1½ cups Chardonnay
3 tablespoons Tomato Relish (recipe follows)
1 pound Yukon Gold, Red Nordland, or White Rose potatoes, diced in ½-inch cubes (2 cups)
Half a red bell pepper, diced (½ cup)
1 onion, peeled and diced (1 cup)
1 teaspoon salt, or more
Freshly ground pepper
1 cup Potato Aioli (recipe follows)
Optional for a main dish:
1½ pounds cod steaks

Scrub the clams and oysters under cold running water with a wire brush.

In a large cooking pot, heat the olive oil, 1 unpeeled garlic clove, and the bay leaf. Add the clams, oysters, and Chardonnay. Cover the pot and bring the wine to a rolling boil. After 5 minutes, remove the open shellfish to a bowl. Discard the shells, reserving a few for decoration. If there are clams or oysters reluctant to open, pry them open! If they smell fresh, they are fine to eat.

Strain the broth, discarding the garlic and bay leaf. Pour the broth back into the pot and add the tomato relish, potatoes, red pepper, onion, and 1 minced garlic clove. Season with 1 teaspoon salt and freshly ground pepper. Taste and correct seasoning. Cover and cook for 20 minutes.

Add the shellfish and reheat for 1 minute. Serve immediately, with the aioli on the side.

Optional: Poach the cod in the chowder for 10 minutes, or until a match stick pierces the flesh of the fish with ease.

Serves 6

TOMATO RELISH

If you have access to great tomatoes, make batches of this relish. It refrigerates for 2 weeks and freezes for at least 6 months before losing its flavor.

1 pound tomatoes (during the winter, substitute one 16-ounce can tomatoes, drained)
½ teaspoon kosher salt
3 tablespoons olive oil
1 garlic clove, peeled and chopped
¼ cup shredded basil in the summer, or ¼ cup shredded parsley in winter

Chop the tomatoes. Sprinkle salt over them and let drain in a colander for ½ hour. Heat the oil with the garlic. Add the tomatoes and the basil or parsley, cover, and simmer for 15 minutes.

Let cool and refrigerate or freeze.

Makes 1 cup

POTATO AIOLI OR ROUILLE

In Provence, aioli (a garlic mayonnaise) is made with an egg or with mashed potatoes. The rouille is an aioli with mashed hot chile peppers. Extra-virgin oil is too strong for this dish, but if that's all you have, mix it with vegetable oil.

Several strands of saffron (optional)
4 large garlic cloves
Salt
1 chile pepper (mandatory for rouille, optional for aioli)
2 tablespoons mashed potatoes
½ cup light olive oil
1 teaspoon lemon juice
Pepper

Dissolve the saffron in 2 tablespoons water (this step is optional; you can make the aioli without the saffron, but you will need the water).

Peel the garlic cloves. (If the garlic is sprouting, slice it open and remove the bitter green sprout in the center.) Mash the garlic into a purée with a pinch of salt. For rouille, mash 1 chile pepper and combine with the garlic.

(continued)

Mix in the mashed potatoes and start whisking in the oil drop by drop, occasionally adding water and lemon juice. Season with salt and pepper.

Makes ⅔ cup

Potato and Red Pepper Soup

- **1 pound russet potatoes, peeled and diced into 1-inch cubes (about 3 cups)**
- **1 red pepper, seeded and diced (1 cup)**
- **1 celery stalk, diced (1 cup)**
- **1 onion, peeled and diced (1 cup)**
- **1 pound chicken or turkey backs, cut up**
- **1 tablespoon salt**
- **Tabasco**

In a stockpot, cover the vegetables and chicken bones with 6 cups cold salted water and bring to a boil. Skim off the scum that rises to the top. Partially cover and simmer until the vegetables are tender, about 1 hour.

Strain into a bowl. Pick through the solids to remove all chicken bones (pick the meat off the bones and set aside for the soup or for sandwiches). Return the vegetables to the broth.

Process the soup in a food processor or through a food mill. Reheat, adding a few drops of Tabasco and more salt, if needed.

Serves 6

Shellfish, Sorrel, and Potato Soup

- 2 dozen mussels and/or small cherrystone clams
- 1 dozen oysters
- 2 pounds Yukon Gold, Red Nordland, or White Rose potatoes, diced into ½-inch cubes (5 cups)
- 2 cups sliced leek whites
- 7 cups chicken stock or water
- 1 tablespoon salt
- 4 cups fine julienne of sorrel or watercress

Scrub the shellfish very well with a small wire brush.

Combine the potatoes, leeks, and 7 cups of chicken stock or water. Add 1 tablespoon salt. Bring to a boil and cover. Simmer until the potatoes are tender, about 20 minutes.

Add the sorrel and the shellfish. Cover and cook until the shellfish open.

Shuck the mollusks, keeping 2 mussels or clams and 1 oyster on the half shell for decoration in each soup plate.

Serve with toasts.

Serves 6

During my childhood I was never very enthusiastic about eating soup. Unfortunately for me, that's what I had every night. My mother would make soup out of the noon dinner leftovers so nothing was wasted. However, on some Friday nights, I had a treat: a soup I liked. I remember she put in potatoes, sorrel, and mussels. Since she had no cookbook to speak of, I have no idea how she made it. So when I knew I would write a cookbook on potatoes, I tried to re-create the flavor of that wonderful soup. Well, you know how childhood memories play tricks on your tastebuds. I tried and tried to taste my youth again, and now I think I have succeeded.

The shellfish I use are clams, mussels, and oysters. In New York, I never get mussels as briny as they should be, but if you have access to very fresh mussels, put them in; otherwise make the soup with small cherrystone clams and oysters.

The sorrel in the soup adds acidity, which marries well with the shellfish. Watercress is a good substitute if sorrel is not available.

Soupe au Pistou

VEGETABLE SOUP WITH BASIL, TOMATO, AND GARLIC

Soupe au pistou is the minestrone of Provence. This soup is made during the summer months when green and white beans are freshly picked; when tomatoes are ripe and very juicy; and when basil is blooming profusely. In Provence, basil is pistou. But pistou is really a mixture of basil, tomatoes, garlic, cheese, and olive oil. In the States, I like to make the soup when I can buy fresh cranberry beans, sometimes called September or October beans. (A nice old lady once told me at the market in New York that I was not buying cranberry beans but old-fashioned Italian beans!) Substitute dried navy beans if you can't find cranberry beans. This soup is a meal in itself. I always invite special friends when I make it—usually Calvin and Alice Trillin in New York.

1 cup dried navy beans, or 2 pounds unshelled fresh cranberry beans (1 cup shelled)
1 pound Red Nordland, White Rose, or Yukon Gold potatoes, peeled and diced into 1/2-inch cubes (2 cups)
1/2 pound green beans, cut crosswise in 1-inch pieces (2 cups)
1 onion, peeled and chopped
1 pound small zucchini, diced (2 cups)
1 1/2 tablespoons salt
Pistou (recipe follows)

If you are cooking dried beans, cover them by 1 inch with cold water and soak overnight. Drain. Cover with cold water and bring to a boil. Drain and reserve for the soup.

In a large pot, cover the vegetables with 8 cups salted cold water and bring to a boil. (The volume of vegetables is more or less equal to the volume of water.) Cover, bring to a boil quickly, and then simmer for 45 minutes.

When the soup is ready, mix in half of the pistou, cover the pot, and let stand for 1 minute. Serve the remaining pistou on the side. Eat with crusty country bread and have a glass or two of sturdy Côtes du Rhône red wine or a zinfandel.

Serves 4 as main dish, 8 as a soup course

PISTOU

1 pound ripe tomatoes
2 cups basil leaves
8 garlic cloves, peeled and coarsely chopped
1/3 cup grated Parmesan
1 cup grated Gruyère
1/3 cup olive oil
Salt and pepper

Drop the tomatoes into boiling water for 30 seconds, then transfer them to a bowl of cold water. Peel, quarter, and squeeze out the juice.

In the bowl of the food processor fitted with the metal blade, combine basil, garlic, and tomatoes. Pulse for 1 minute and gradually and alternately add the cheeses and dribble in 1/4 cup olive oil. Pulse for another minute or until all the ingredients are mixed, stopping 2 or 3 times to scrape the sides of the bowl. If too thick, dribble in the rest of the olive oil. Add salt and pepper to taste.

German Potato Soup with Meat and Spaetzle

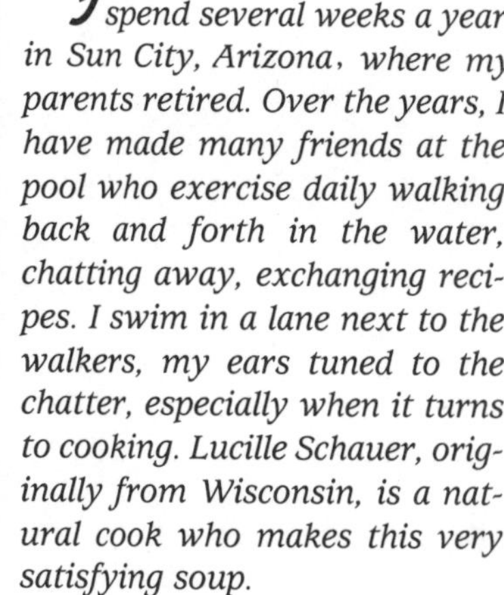

I spend several weeks a year in Sun City, Arizona, where my parents retired. Over the years, I have made many friends at the pool who exercise daily walking back and forth in the water, chatting away, exchanging recipes. I swim in a lane next to the walkers, my ears tuned to the chatter, especially when it turns to cooking. Lucille Schauer, originally from Wisconsin, is a natural cook who makes this very satisfying soup.

1 pound shoulder pork chops with bones, cubed
1 pound beef stew meat, cubed
1 tablespoon salt
1 onion, peeled and chopped (1 cup)
2 pounds Yukon Gold, Red Nordland, or White Rose potatoes, peeled and cubed (5 cups)
Spaetzle (page 32)

In a saucepan, cover the meats with 6 cups salted water and bring to a boil. Skim off the scum on top, cover the pan, and simmer for 1 to 2 hours, depending on the quality of the meat, until tender. Set aside to cool, and degrease the broth.

Add the onion and potatoes to the broth. If there is not enough broth, add more water to cover the meat and vegetables. Bring to a boil and cook until the potatoes are tender, about 20 minutes.

At the last minute, cook the spaetzle in the soup. Serve immediately.

Serves 6

There is on the market a spaetzle machine; however, a colander will do the job. The bigger the holes of the colander, the bigger the spaetzle will be.

You need to work very fast when you are pushing the spaetzle dough through the holes of the colander, otherwise the steam of the boiling water underneath will cook the spaetzle and plug the holes of the colander.

SPAETZLE

1 large egg
Salt and freshly ground pepper
2/3 cup all-purpose flour

In a large bowl, mix the egg, 1/3 cup water, salt, and pepper. Gradually whisk in the flour, making a smooth batter.

Set aside for 1 hour.

Pour the spaetzle batter into a colander and hold it right over the boiling soup. With a rubber spatula, push the dough through the holes very quickly so the steam does not cook the dough in the holes of the colander.

When the spaetzle rise back to the surface, cook for 30 seconds. Serve the soup immediately with good country bread.

Serves 6

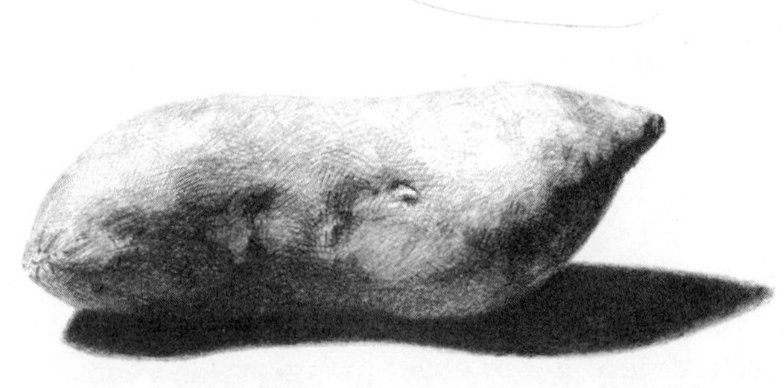

Sweet Potato Soup

- 1 ½ pounds sweet potatoes, peeled and diced into 1-inch cubes (5 cups)
- ½ pound russet baking potatoes, peeled and diced into 1-inch cubes (1 ½ cups)
- 1 onion, peeled and diced (½ cup)
- 1 pound chicken or turkey backs, cut up
- 1 ½ tablespoons salt
- Freshly ground black pepper
- ¼ cup cream (optional)

Not only is this soup good to eat, it is lovely to look at. It will remind you of pumpkin soup. November and December are the best months to buy sweet potatoes.

In a stockpot, cover the vegetables and the chicken or turkey backs with 8 cups cold salted water and bring to a slow boil. Partially cover and cook for 1 hour.

Discard the bones (pick out the meat and set aside for sandwiches).

Process the vegetables until smooth, gradually adding 2 cups of broth. Return the soup to a pan and whisk in 4 cups of the remaining broth for a medium thick soup. Reheat and when the soup is very hot, taste and correct seasoning. Refrigerate any remaining broth for your next soup.

Ladle the soup into individual soup plates and dribble ½ tablespoon heavy cream onto each portion. Serve at once.

Serves 8

Louis Diat, the French-born chef of the now defunct Ritz Carlton in New York City, created this wonderful cold summer soup. His inspiration was the classic French leek and potato soup that his mother made in the hamlet of Montmaraut, near the city of Vichy. Vichy is famous for its mineral water and spa, and infamous as the seat of the French government under Nazi rule during World War II.

Long before World War II, Louis Diat named his creation Vichyssoise, a cool treat for his summer diners at the Ritz when air-conditioning did not exist.

Vichyssoise

- 4 tablespoons (1/2 stick) unsalted butter
- 4 leeks, white part only, thinly sliced (3 1/2 cups)
- 1 medium onion, peeled and thinly sliced (2/3 cup)
- 1 tablespoon salt
- 1 1/2 pounds russet potatoes, peeled and thinly sliced (4 cups)
- 4 cups chicken stock
- 2 cups milk
- 2 cups half and half
- White pepper
- 1/2 cup heavy cream
- 1/4 cup minced fresh chives

Melt the butter in a heavy-bottomed pan or a dutch oven. Add the leeks and onion and cook for 5 minutes, stirring occasionally to prevent scorching. Sprinkle with 1 teaspoon salt.

Stir in the potatoes. Cook for 1 minute. Add the chicken stock and the remaining 2 teaspoons salt. Cover and simmer for 30 minutes.

Ladle by ladle, rub the potatoes, leeks, and onion through a strainer, using the back of a spoon to force the mixture through. This step is very important; don't try to go faster by throwing all the vegetables in the strainer at once—it won't work. Just take your time. This is essential for the texture. M. Diat used a tamis (drum sieve), but a regular kitchen strainer is adequate. You can speed the process a bit by using a food mill. Don't, though, be tempted to use a processor—it will ruin the texture.

Return the mixture to the pan with 2 cups of milk and 2 cups half and half. Bring to a boil and boil for 1 minute.

Strain once more through the strainer, rubbing against it to force lumps through. The soup will have a silky texture, the mark of a true vichyssoise.

Chill the soup, soup bowls, and soup spoons overnight.

When ready to serve, taste the soup and correct seasoning with salt and white pepper, if necessary. Pour into the chilled soup bowls, dribble 1 tablespoon of cream on top of each serving and sprinkle with chives. Serve immediately.

Serves 8 to 10

Leek and Potato Soup

This is an everyday soup in France. In many households, the soup is made with water. When it is served, a pat of butter or margarine is added to enhance the flavors of the vegetables.

- **4 tablespoons (½ stick) unsalted butter or margarine**
- **4 leeks, tough green leaves removed, sliced (4 cups)**
- **1½ pounds russet potatoes, peeled and sliced (4 cups)**
- **6 cups unsalted chicken stock**
- **1 tablespoon salt**
- **6 tablespoons (¾ stick) unsalted butter or margarine (optional)**

Melt the 4 tablespoons butter in a heavy-bottomed pan or a dutch oven. Add the leeks and potatoes and sauté the vegetables for 5 minutes, stirring occasionally to prevent scorching.

Add the chicken stock or water and salt. (If the chicken stock is salted, add only 1 teaspoon of salt.) Bring to a boil, cover, and cook for 35 minutes.

Place a tablespoon of butter or margarine in each bowl if the soup was made with water. Serve immediately.

Serves 6

Potato Soup for Waistline-Watchers

I could not resist making this soup when my friend Elizabeth Herz gave me this recipe from a German Swiss cookbook she swears by, Meisterhaft Kochen, *written by Agnes Amberg, who owns and cooks in her restaurant in Zurich. I listen to Elizabeth because I know she is a terrific cook. "Kartoffelsuppe für Linienbewußte" is an excellent soup.*

2 tablespoons unsalted butter, or oil
1 onion, peeled and chopped (1 cup)
1½ pounds russet potatoes, peeled and diced into 1-inch cubes (4 cups)
Several sprigs fresh parsley
1 sprig marjoram
1 sprig thyme
8 cups unsalted chicken stock
5 teaspoons salt
Freshly ground nutmeg
1 cup plain yogurt

FOR GARNISH:

2 tablespoons unsalted butter
½ cup minced shallots

Melt the butter or oil in a dutch oven; sauté the onion and potatoes for 3 minutes. Add the herbs and sauté for another minute.

Add the stock and salt (if the stock is salted, add only 2 teaspoons of salt). Bring to a boil and simmer for 30 minutes, or until the potatoes are fork tender.

Purée the vegetables in a blender or food processor. Return to the pan with the nutmeg and yogurt. Taste and correct seasoning.

Meanwhile, melt the butter in a nonstick skillet and sauté the shallots for 1 minute. Reheat the soup with the sautéed shallots. Serve immediately.

Serves 8

Après-Ski Soup

4 tablespoons (½ stick) butter or margarine
1 onion, peeled and diced (1 cup)
1 large garlic clove, peeled and chopped
½ pound russet potatoes, peeled and diced into ½-inch cubes (1 cup)
1½ pounds white turnips, peeled and diced into ½-inch cubes (3 cups)
1 parsnip, peeled and diced into ½-inch cubes (1 cup)
4 cups chicken broth, or 4 cups water and 1 pound chicken backs, cut up
2 teaspoons salt
Freshly ground pepper
½ cup sour cream (optional)
½ cup whipping cream (optional)
1 cup plain yogurt (optional)
8 drops Tabasco

Gloria Karlitz, one of my student friends, created this delicious soup for an après-ski snack. If you are not skiing and do not want to make the soup so rich, substitute plain yogurt for sour cream and cream.

Melt the butter or margarine in a dutch oven. Sauté the onion and garlic for 1 minute. Cover and braise over low heat for 10 minutes.

Uncover the pot, raise the heat, toss in the rest of the vegetables, and stir-fry for 5 minutes.

Add the broth (or water with chicken backs), salt, and freshly ground pepper. Cover and simmer until tender (about 30 minutes).

If necessary pick out the chicken bones and meat. Purée the soup in a blender or food processor.

Reheat the soup with sour cream and cream (or yogurt). Sprinkle with several drops of Tabasco, taste and correct seasoning, and serve immediately.

Serves 6

3.
Potato Salads

For salads, choose a potato variety based on the texture you like for the finished salad. For American potato salad, I want a potato that partly crumbles when cubed, so I use an all-purpose potato. For German potato salad, I grate a boiled baking potato. For salade Niçoise, I want a firm texture so I steam freshly dug new potatoes, or the red potato varieties.

Always buy potatoes of the same size for boiling or steaming, so they will cook evenly and not become waterlogged. Always cook them in their jackets, to help keep them intact while cooking.

As soon as the potatoes are cooked, peel them steaming hot, cut them, and sprinkle with vinegar or white wine. Hot potatoes will absorb flavors; cold potatoes will not.

When I make potato salad, I am always reminded of the charming story in *Rules of the Game*, Jean Renoir's classic movie about the loves and intrigues of the upper class and their servants. In the kitchen of the chateau, the servants are eating and gossiping about the true pedigree of their boss, the Marquis de LaCheney. The chef, who has heard enough gossip, suddenly speaks up for his boss, showing respect for a man who knows how a potato salad should taste: "LaCheney, even if he is not a blueblood, called me the other day to chew me out about a potato salad. As you know, or rather you don't know, in order for the salad to be edible, the white wine must be poured over the potatoes when they are still absolutely boiling hot. Celestin did not do this because he does not like to burn his fingers. Well, the boss sniffed that right away. You can say what you want, but that shows him to be a man of the world."

I wear thick oven mittens to peel the potatoes, because, like Celestin, I don't like to burn my fingers while peeling hot potatoes.

American Potato Salad

My friend Nadine Stewart is proud of her mother's potato salad: "My mother is not a gourmet cook and never wanted to be, but she thinks of herself as one of the best makers of potato salad and feels confident she's never had one to equal hers. It's a small specialty, but it's enough for her. She made big bowls of it in the summer when we went on picnics. She cooked the potatoes in the morning, seasoned the steaming potatoes, and let them sit and absorb the

4 pounds all-purpose (Superior, Kennebec) potatoes
1/3 cup red wine vinegar
1 tablespoon sugar
1/2 cup finely chopped onion
1 1/2 teaspoons salt
Freshly ground pepper
1 cup diced celery
1 cup diced green pepper
1 tablespoon celery seeds
1 1/2 cups mayonnaise
2 hard-boiled eggs, sliced
1/8 teaspoon hot paprika

In a large pot or a stockpot, cover the potatoes with a generous amount of salted cold water. Bring to a boil, cover, and cook for 40 minutes, or until tender.

Drain and peel the hot potatoes (put on a thick kitchen mitten to avoid burning your fingers) and cut into 1-inch cubes. You should have about 10 cups of potatoes.

Pour the vinegar mixed with the sugar over the hot potatoes, add the onion and season with salt and freshly ground pepper. Set aside for 1 hour.

Toss the celery, green pepper, and celery seeds into the potatoes with your hands. Mix in the mayonnaise. Taste and correct seasoning. Decorate the top of the salad with the eggs and sprinkle with paprika.

Serves 8

vinegar and the other flavorings. The texture of the potato salad is between firm and crumbly. . . . My brother Bruce was allowed to draw up the menu for his birthday on December 15; he always chose potato salad . . . he wanted a winter picnic. I can still remember all the little boys gobbling the whole big red bowl of salad."

La Salade du Berger

THE SHEPHERD'S SALAD

The French make a similar salad, decorated like a clock face. For the face of the clock, smooth out the top of the salad with mayonnaise, decorate the borders with half slices of tomatoes, and make roman numerals and the hands of the clock with green beans or haricots verts.

Madame Bauve's Hot Potato Salad

Madame Adrienne Bauve, a ninety-year-old, is known to be the champion maker of potato salads in the Ardennes, a province in northeastern France, next to Belgium. Her grandchildren remember the days when grandmi *made great batches of potato salad at a time and invited family and friends for potato salad dinners. Her husband was the only family member who refused to eat it until one day he tasted leftovers at his sister's. He ate without commenting on it. From that time on, he ate potato salad without ever acknowledging how good it was, to the despair of his wife; but like all stubborn husbands, he did not want to admit how wrong he had been.*

4 pounds russet or Yukon Gold potatoes
1 head chicory lettuce
1 pound lean bacon, rind removed, cut into ½-inch pieces
½ cup milk, or more
¼ cup red wine vinegar
2 large garlic cloves, peeled and minced
Salt and pepper

In a saucepan, cover the potatoes with a large amount of cold salted water and bring to a boil. Partially cover and cook for 35 minutes, or until tender.

Meanwhile, wash and dry the salad leaves. With a pair of scissors, cut the greens into small shreds. Place in a 9-quart dutch oven.

Cook the bacon in a skillet until crisp. Drain on paper towels and reserve ½ cup bacon fat in the skillet.

Drain the potatoes and peel. Purée them directly over the salad greens through a food mill fitted with a coarse blade, or mash the potatoes with an old-fashioned masher. With either implement, add enough milk to moisten the potatoes as you are mashing them.

Toss in the bacon and pour in the reserved bacon fat. Deglaze the skillet with ¼ cup wine vinegar over high heat, scraping the bottom of the pan. Pour over the potatoes.

Toss the salad greens, potatoes, bacon, and garlic together. Taste and season with salt and freshly ground pepper.

Reheat over medium heat for 5 minutes, wilting the salad leaves. Serve immediately.

Serves 10

German Potato Salad with Onions and Bacon

4 pounds russet potatoes
1 pound lean bacon, rind removed, cut into ½-inch pieces
2 medium onions, peeled and chopped
2 garlic cloves, peeled and minced
½ cup rich chicken stock
⅓ cup distilled white vinegar
5 tablespoons minced fresh parsley
About 2 teaspoons salt

FOR THE GARNISH:

Several salad leaves

In a saucepan, cover the potatoes in cold salted water and bring to a boil. Partially cover and cook for 35 minutes, or until tender.

In a large skillet, cook the bacon until crisp, stirring occasionally. Set aside ¼ of the bacon for the garnish.

Add the onions and the garlic to the remaining bacon in the skillet and cook until the onions are softened but not browned, 8 to 10 minutes, stirring occasionally.

Add the chicken stock and vinegar. Increase the heat and boil the liquids. Set aside.

Peel the potatoes hot and cut them in ½-inch cubes. In a large bowl, combine the steaming potatoes and the onion-bacon dressing. Toss the potato salad with ¼ cup parsley and salt. Taste and correct seasoning.

Set aside for at least 1 or 2 hours before eating, to let the flavors mingle.

To serve, invert the potato salad onto a serving platter. Garnish with greens. Sprinkle the top of the potatoes with the reserved bacon and the remaining tablespoon of parsley.

Serves 8

This salad is a meal in itself and is better the day after it's made. It's a good winter buffet dish.

This heads the list of potato salads made with firm-textured (waxy) potatoes, peeled steaming hot and sprinkled with white wine.

Salade Niçoise

1 sprig fresh tarragon
2 pounds unpeeled small Red La Rouge, Ruby Crescent, or small Yukon Gold potatoes
⅔ cup white wine
One 6-ounce can chunk tuna in oil
8 or more anchovy fillets, chopped
1 teaspoon salt
Freshly ground pepper
½ pound tender green beans or haricots verts, ends trimmed and cut in half crosswise
2 large garlic cloves, peeled and minced
2 tablespoons wine vinegar
½ cup olive oil
½ cup niçoises olives
½ pound tomatoes, cubed

Pour about 1 inch of water in the bottom of a large pan, add the fresh tarragon, and bring to a boil.

Fit a steamer in the boiling water and steam the potatoes whole for 15 to 20 minutes, depending on their size and variety.

Quickly peel the hot potatoes. Cut them in 1-inch cubes and pour over the white wine while the potatoes are still steaming hot. Drain the tuna and toss it and the anchovies into the potatoes. Sprinkle with salt and grind over fresh pepper; set aside.

Bring a large amount of water to a boil, add the green beans or haricots verts, and bring back to a boil; add ½ teaspoon salt and cook until slightly crunchy but not raw (about 2 to 3 minutes).

Meanwhile in a large salad bowl, whisk garlic, vinegar, and oil together. Drain the beans and quickly toss them in the oil mixture.

Finally, toss the potato salad into the green beans. It can be prepared several hours before serving.

At the last minute, scatter olives and tomatoes over the salad and mix. Taste and correct seasoning if necessary.

Serves 4

An Elegant Potato Salad

1½ pounds unpeeled small Red La Rouge, Ruby Crescent, Peruvian Blue, or Yukon Gold potatoes
½ cup white wine
Salt
Freshly ground pepper
1 tablespoon minced fresh tarragon
1 ounce (1 cup) dry morels
2 tablespoons butter or margarine
1 small head radicchio, cut into fine julienne (2 cups)
1 small fennel bulb, cut into fine julienne (2 cups)
4½ ounces Gruyère cheese, cut into fine julienne (1 cup)
½ cup Vinaigrette Dressing (page 52)
4 cups watercress, stems removed
4 cups arugula, stems removed
1 tablespoon walnut oil
½ tablespoon vinegar

I served this potato salad at the beginning of a summer dinner party for ten people. It was a great hit. For the look more than the taste, steam a few Peruvian Blue potatoes with the other potato varieties you choose for the salad.

Pour about 1 inch of water into a large pan. Bring to a boil, fit the steamer into the pan, put in the potatoes, cover, and steam for 15 to 20 minutes, depending on the size of the potatoes (Peruvian Blues will take longer to cook).

Peel the hot potatoes and cut into ½-inch slices, or quarter them if they are very small. Pour the wine over them and sprinkle with salt, freshly ground pepper, and tarragon.

Meanwhile, soak the morels in 1 cup water for half an hour. Drain through paper towels and reserve the liquid.

Quarter the morels only if they are more than 1 inch long. Heat 2 tablespoons butter and sauté the morels for a minute, then gradually add the morel liquid over high heat and boil it down until 2 or 3 tablespoons remain. Season with salt and pepper and toss morels and the reduced liquid with the potatoes.

Stack the leaves of the radicchio and roll up like a cigarette. Cut crosswise into very thin strips. You should have about 2 cups.

Toss the radicchio, fennel, and cheese into the potato salad and

(continued)

mix in the vinaigrette dressing. Taste and add more salt and pepper if necessary.

Decorate each plate with watercress and arugula, sprinkle oil and vinegar over the greens, and fill the center with potato salad.

Serves 10

I always keep my ears open when I hear about So-and-so's potato salad as the best potato salad they ever ate. Elaine Snyder, a fashion stylist living in Los Angeles, has all her friends talking about her potato salad with good reason; it's delicious and it improves the next day.

Potato Salad with Cucumbers and Red Onion

3 pounds Red Pontiac or Nordland potatoes
1/4 cup minced chives
1 cup mayonnaise
2 teaspoons salt
Freshly ground pepper
2 cups thinly sliced peeled cucumber
1 cup thinly sliced peeled red onion

In a large saucepan, cover the potatoes with cold salted water and bring to a boil. Partially cover and cook for 30 minutes, or until tender.

In a large bowl, mix the chives, 2/3 cup mayonnaise, 1 teaspoon of the salt, and freshly ground pepper.

Drain and peel the steaming potatoes. Cut them into 1/4-inch-thick slices and toss them into the mayonnaise.

Toss the cucumber slices with 1/4 cup mayonnaise and sprinkle with the remaining 1 teaspoon salt, and pepper. Toss the onion with the remaining mayonnaise.

Fill a glass bowl with layers of potatoes, cucumbers, and onion. Refrigerate until ready to serve.

Serves 6

Salad of Potatoes with Shellfish

2 pounds mussels
2 pounds small cherrystone clams
5 tablespoons olive oil
¼ cup red wine vinegar
⅓ cup minced shallots
1½ pounds small Yukon Gold, Red La Rouge, Ruby Crescent, or Peruvian Blue potatoes, unpeeled
¼ cup minced parsley
Salt

Scrub the mussels thoroughly under cold water and steam them in a large pot with ½ cup of water. Cover the pot and steam over medium heat until they open, about 3 minutes. Strain the broth through cheesecloth and set aside broth and mussels separately.

Scrub the clams carefully and steam them in the same pot, covered, with ½ cup of water. Steam over medium heat until they open, about 5 minutes. Strain the broth through cheesecloth. Set aside the clams and broth.

Add the olive oil, 2 tablespoons of the vinegar, and the minced shallots to the combined broths. Boil down to half, or until very tasty.

Meanwhile, pour about 1 inch of water into a large pan and bring to a boil. Fit a steamer in the pan, put in the potatoes, cover, and steam for 15 to 20 minutes, depending on their size and varieties.

Peel the steaming hot potatoes, cut them into cubes, and sprinkle with the remaining 2 tablespoons vinegar and the minced parsley.

Simmer the shellfish broth and toss the shellfish and the hot broth over the potatoes. Taste and correct seasoning.

Serves 6

Jean Luc Abras is a musician who likes to putter in the kitchen. He invited us for a flute concert and for his potato salad. Both were wonderful.

Potato and Lentil Salad with Boiled Sausage

Potato and lentil salad is on the menu of most bistros in Lyon, the gastronomical capital of France. The salad is basic and very easy to make, but the ingredients must be first quality. Green lentils are found in specialty shops, such as Todaro Brothers, 557 Second Avenue, New York, NY 10016. In Lyon, big fat garlic sausages are boiled and served with the potatoes and lentils. I make a meal of this salad, serving Dijon mustard and tart small gherkins with it. I finish the meal with a platter of cheese and fruits.

1 1/4 cup green lentils
1 onion, peeled and quartered
1 carrot, peeled and cut in chunks
2 garlic cloves, peeled and coarsely chopped
1 teaspoon dried thyme, or 1 sprig fresh thyme
1 tablespoon plus 1 teaspoon salt
2 pounds unpeeled Yukon Gold, Red La Rouge, or White Rose potatoes
3/4 pound French garlic sausage, or German, Polish, or Italian sausage
1 1/4 cup Vinaigrette Dressing (page 52)
3 tablespoons white wine
3 tablespoons olive oil
Freshly ground pepper

Soak the lentils in a large amount of water for 1 hour. Drain. In a 6-quart saucepan, cover the lentils, onion, carrot, garlic, thyme, and 1 tablespoon salt with 4 cups of water. Bring to a boil. Cover and simmer until the lentils are cooked, about 45 minutes to 1 hour.

Cover the potatoes with cold salted water and bring to a boil. Partially cover and cook for 30 to 40 minutes, or until tender.

Meanwhile, cover the sausage with water and bring to a boil. Boil until tender, about 30 minutes (the time will depend on the thickness of the sausage).

Drain the lentils if necessary. Discard the carrot and onion. Mix in the vinaigrette dressing and set aside.

Peel the steaming potatoes and cut them into 1/2-inch-thick slices. Pour the white wine and oil over them. Sprinkle with 1 teaspoon salt and freshly ground pepper. Set aside.

Peel the sausage and cut into 1/2-inch-thick slices. On each plate, place a mound of lentils, a mound of potatoes, and 2 slices of sausage, overlapping. Serve warm or at room temperature.

Serves 4

Winter Mixed Salad

4 ounces goat cheese, crumbled (1 cup)
½ cup Vinaigrette Dressing (recipe follows)
½ cup coarsely chopped walnuts
1 pound all-purpose (Superior, Kennebec) potatoes, peeled and cut into ½-inch cubes (3 cups)
½ teaspoon salt
Freshly ground pepper
2 tablespoons oil
¼ pound lean bacon
2 slices French bread, cut into ½-inch-thick slices and then into ½-inch cubes, and dried in the oven
1 large garlic clove, peeled and cut in half
1 head chicory lettuce, washed and dried

Combine the crumbled cheese with the vinaigrette and the walnuts.

Cook the potatoes in cold salted water for 15 minutes, or until tender. Drain and toss in the vinaigrette mixture while the potatoes are still hot. Season with salt and freshly ground pepper.

Heat the oil in a large skillet and add the bacon strips. Brown evenly without burning. When the bacon is crisp, crumble and toss it into the potatoes.

Brown the croutons in the skillet, adding more oil if necessary. Rub a garlic clove over the surface of the croutons.

Toss the chicory and the croutons in the potato salad. Taste and correct seasoning, adding more vinaigrette dressing if necessary.

Serves 4

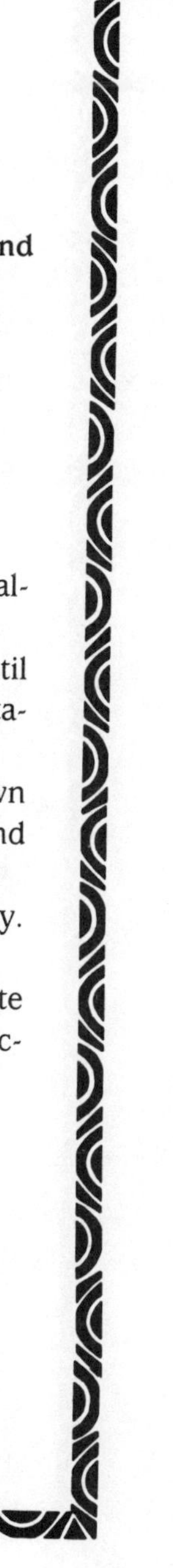

Vinaigrette Dressing

1 teaspoon salt
Freshly ground pepper
1 teaspoon prepared Dijon-style mustard
1 tablespoon red wine vinegar
¼ cup olive or sunflower oil
2 tablespoons walnut oil

Place salt and pepper in a mixing bowl. Add the mustard and mix in the vinegar. Add the oils and whisk vigorously. Taste and correct seasoning.

Makes ½ cup

Summer Potato Salad

2 red peppers
2 pounds small Red La Rouge, Yukon Gold, or Yellow Finnish potatoes
1½ teaspoons salt
2 tablespoons red wine vinegar
3 tablespoons walnut oil
3 tablespoons olive oil
4 ounces *chèvre* or feta cheese, crumbled (1 cup)
½ pound young green beans or haricots verts, ends snapped off
8 large basil leaves
Salad greens

Char the peppers on gas burners or under the broiler on an electric stove, turning them once in a while with tongs. Transfer them to a sturdy plastic bag, tie, and set aside.

Pour 1 inch of water into a large pan and bring to a boil. Fit a steamer in the pan and put in the potatoes, cover, and steam for 15 to 20 minutes, depending on the size and the varieties of the potatoes.

In a large bowl, mix salt, 1½ tablespoons of the vinegar, 2 tablespoons of the walnut oil, and the olive oil. Crumble the cheese into the dressing.

A few minutes before the potatoes are tender, boil a large amount of salted water and drop in the beans for 2 minutes, or long enough to cook away their raw crunch. (The potatoes and beans should be ready simultaneously to be seasoned while still hot.)

Peel the steaming potatoes hot and cut into ¼-inch slices; toss them in the dressing. Drain the beans and add them to the potatoes.

With your hands, shred the basil leaves on top of the vegetables, and toss the potatoes, beans, and basil together in the dressing.

Peel the peppers and remove the stems, seeds, and inner ribs. Slice the peppers into thin julienne strips. Toss them into the potato salad. Taste and correct seasoning if necessary.

Garnish salad plates with the greens and sprinkle with the remaining 1½ teaspoons vinegar and 1 tablespoon walnut oil. Put the potato salad on top and serve.

Serves 6 for an appetizer, 4 for lunch

Barbecued Potato Salad

In the summer, Joe Ciccone is master chef at the grill in his backyard. Barbara, his wife, marinates the potatoes in olive oil and rosemary, and Joe prepares the grill. It's a worthwhile team effort, as their roasted potatoes are excellent, basted with the marinade mixture and served with a splash of white vinegar.

2 pounds small Red La Rouge, baby Yukon Gold, or Ruby Crescent potatoes
2 sprigs fresh rosemary
½ cup fruity olive oil
2 tablespoons white wine vinegar
Salt
Freshly ground pepper

Split the potatoes in two (for the Ruby Crescents, split lengthwise). Score the cut faces of each potato.

In a pan large enough to hold all the potatoes, mix the oil and the rosemary. Place the potatoes in the pan, cut sides down. Set aside for 2 hours.

Baste the potato jackets with oil from the marinade before placing over the hot coals of a grill. Roast them cut side down first, for 3 or 4 minutes, watching that the potatoes do not burn. Invert them with tongs and roast until the potatoes are brown but not burned, and fork tender.

Cut each half in chunks. Sprinkle with vinegar and the remaining oil from the marinade. Serve warm with salt and pepper on the side.

Serves 4

4.
Breads

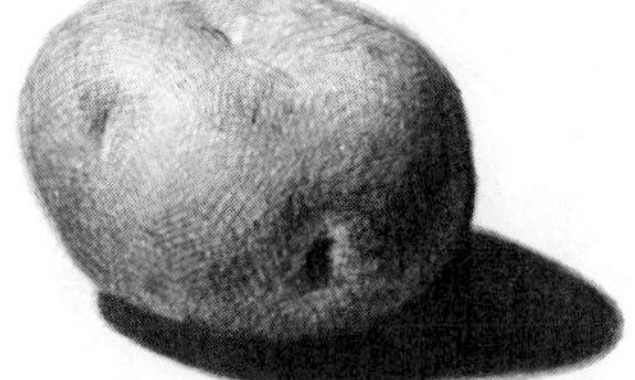

Potato bread is magic to me, and I will always associate it with baseball. I need to explain. I came to the United States from France in the early fifties when I was fifteen years old. During the war, French bakers made bread with whatever they could put their hands on. Generally, it was not wheat flour but flour made from feed corn! I still remember the taste of this awful bread. But for a young Parisian, bread came and still comes from a bakery, and not from mom's oven. I lived in Ohio those first years, and many of my friends' mothers made bread, especially potato bread, that smelled heavenly. How I wish I had learned then to make it, but my friends and I were too busy watching the Cleveland Indians trying to beat those damned Yankees. Baseball was my passion. And during that fateful year of 1954 when the Indians lost four straight games in the World Series to the New York Giants, my baseball buddies and I would eat freshly made potato bread with frankfurters doused in mustard, all washed down with chocolate milkshakes. The bread was cake and brioche in one; a treat for a French girl who had eaten miserable cornbread during the war.

POTATO BREAD

The ideal potato for bread is the russet, the Idaho potato. High in starch, it is the most floury and the least moist—qualities essential for bread-making. If you have only all-purpose potatoes in the house and want to use them, use about 1/4 less liquid, or about 1 cup more flour than called for in the bread recipe. It will work.

Choose small russet potatoes and cook them whole, unpeeled. Small potatoes cook evenly, quickly, and do not become waterlogged. The peel gives flavor to the cooking water, which is used for the sponge (the yeast mixture). Drain the potatoes as soon as they are cooked; otherwise, they get waterlogged and gluey.

Potato bread is made with mashed potatoes, flour, yeast, and potato water, which is sometimes combined with milk. Most recipes for potato bread are written for seven to eight loaves because it keeps practically forever in the refrigerator and is excellent for sandwiches and toasts. I have cut down the recipes to two or three loaves of bread, making it easier to handle. All the bread recipes in this chapter ask for 1 1/4 pounds potatoes, about 3 medium-sized potatoes.

The amount of flour incorporated in the bread dough depends on two major factors: the percentage of protein in the flour and the percentage of humidity in the weather. I use an all-purpose flour with 12 percent protein and a bread flour with 14 percent protein (the percentage of protein is written on the side of the flour bag); the lower the percentage, the more flour is needed in bread making.

When the weather is humid, I add more flour than stated in the bread recipes and when I make bread in Arizona, a state with low humidity, I incorporate flour very slowly in the dough but I never add more flour than is mentioned in the recipe.

I buy active dry yeast in bulk in health food stores and I keep it in the freezer for several months. It is much cheaper than buying individual 2-teaspoon packages. If you prefer using fresh cake yeast, remember that 1/2 ounce of fresh yeast represents 2 teaspoons active dry yeast.

Eliza Acton, nineteenth-century English cookbook writer, stated in *English Bread Book for Domestic Use* (1857), that potato bread "is one of the best varieties of mixed or cheap bread when it is made with care, as its flavour is excellent, and it remains moist longer than any other except rice-bread; but the potatoes used for it should be good, thoroughly boiled, well dried afterwards by having the water poured from them, and then standing by the side of the fire to steam and be reduced to a perfect paste by mashing or be rubbed quickly through a colander or other coarse strainer. They should be perfectly mixed with the flour while they are still warm and after the addition of rather more salt than common bread, the dough, which will require less liquid than wheaten-dough, should be made up smoothly and firmly and be managed afterward like other bread, but be baked in a more gentle oven."

I make bread in a heavy-duty mixer for convenience and speed, but a large bowl, a wooden spoon, and plenty of elbow grease is all you actually need.

I love this bread so much that it takes the place of brioche in my household. I agree with Dr. A. Hunter, who wrote in Receipts in Modern Cookery *(1805) that "lovers of toast and butter will be much pleased with this kind of bread. The potato is not here added with a view to economy, but to increase the lightness of the bread, in which state it will imbibe the butter with more freedom . . ." That's a man after my own heart. For breakfast, for lunch, for dinner, I slice the bread, lightly butter each slice (or dribble on a smidgen of olive oil), and toast it under the broiler on one side.*

Eliza Acton's Potato Bread

1¼ pounds russet potatoes
½ cup milk
2 teaspoons active dry yeast
1 teaspoon sugar
4 cups or more all-purpose flour
1 tablespoon salt

In a saucepan, cover the unpeeled potatoes with cold salted water and bring to a boil. Partially cover and cook for 30 minutes, or until tender.

Preheat the oven to 300 degrees.

Drain the potatoes, reserving ½ cup potato water. Add ½ cup cold milk to the potato water. Sprinkle the yeast and sugar over this liquid and set aside in a warm place for 15 minutes.

Put the potatoes in the oven to dry for 10 minutes.

Peel the potatoes and mash them with a potato masher, ricer, or through a strainer, 1 potato at a time. You should have about 2⅓ to 3 cups mashed potatoes, not packed. Set aside to cool.

Add salt to the flour and mix.

Transfer the yeast mixture to the bowl of a heavy-duty mixer fitted with a flat paddle. Gradually beat in the mashed potatoes, and then add the flour, ¼ cup at a time at first, then tablespoon by tablespoon when the dough sticks to the beater and cleans the bowl. Continue adding flour until all 4 cups are incorporated (about 10 to 15 minutes). Knead in more flour if the dough is very sticky. To combine by hand, stir in the flour with a wooden spoon; when the dough gets too stiff to stir, knead with your hands.

Transfer the dough to a floured work surface and knead with more flour for 1 minute, or until smooth. Return dough to a clean large bowl and cover with a plastic bag (I use supermarket plastic bags for this).

Let rise at room temperature until the dough has doubled in size.

Sprinkle flour on the risen dough and knead it for about 1 minute, adding more flour. It should be a very soft dough.

Butter two 8-cup loaf pans. Cut the dough in two equal parts. With more flour shape each one into a sausagelike roll that will fit nicely in the greased pan. Cover the pans with a large plastic bag and let them rise almost to the tops of the pans.

Preheat the oven to 350 degrees.

Bake the loaves for 50 minutes or until golden brown. Unmold on baking racks.

When the loaves of bread are cold, wrap them in plastic bags and refrigerate. Potato bread lasts several weeks in the refrigerator; the bread stays very moist.

Makes 2 pounds unrisen dough (about 4 cups), to fill two 8-cup loaf pans

Sandwich Monte Cristo

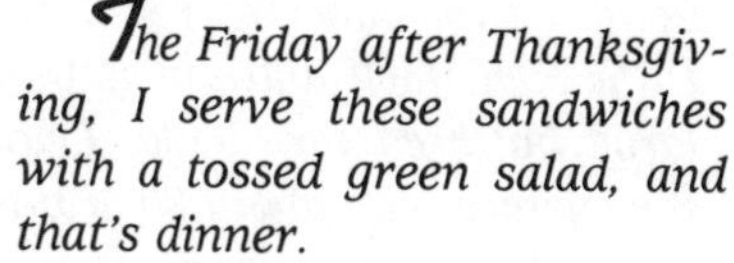

The Friday after Thanksgiving, I serve these sandwiches with a tossed green salad, and that's dinner.

- **1 ½ tablespoons Dijon-style mustard**
- **8 slices Eliza Acton's Potato Bread (page 60), toasted**
- **4 thin slices prosciutto**
- **4 slices cooked turkey or chicken**
- **Salt**
- **Freshly ground pepper**
- **4 slices Swiss cheese**
- **½ cup mayonnaise**

Spread mustard on each slice of bread. Build a sandwich with 1 slice of prosciutto, a slice of leftover turkey or chicken, salt, pepper, a slice of cheese, and one more slice of bread.

Spread 1 tablespoon of mayonnaise on the outside of both pieces of bread in each sandwich. Brown the sandwiches in a nonstick skillet, turning once. Cover the skillet and cook over low heat for 2 or 3 minutes to melt the cheese.

Drain on paper towels. Serve with a tossed green salad.

Serves 4

Gateau Beurre

SWISS BREAD

When I read this recipe in a transcription of Edouard de Pomiane's radio cooking show "Radio Cuisine," I had to try it instantly. I knew it was a winner and I was right. Dr. de Pomiane, a master storyteller, delighted thousands of radio listeners in the 1930s; he held a running conversation with his listeners, giving recipes and talking about the different cultures and cuisines of all the countries he had visited.

This is his recipe for gateau beurre, a specialty of Switzerland: "I buy 400 grams of bread dough at the bakery. I roll it out to 1/8-inch thick and put it in a large buttered tart mold. I dot the surface with about 80 grams of butter. I salt it, pepper it, and bake it in a hot oven for 10 minutes. I remove it from the oven and I cut a kind of pancake in butter-sloshed wedges. Slosh is not a very scientific name but this butter pancake is an admirable find."

When I make Eliza Acton's bread, I reserve a piece of dough for gateau beurre. I refrigerate it until 1 hour before baking, having left the dough in the refrigerator for as long as 1 week. Eat it hot, right out of the oven, with a soup or a tossed salad.

An 11-inch pan with removable bottom

10 ounces (about 1 1/3 cups) Eliza Acton's Bread dough (page 60)
6 tablespoons (3/4 stick) butter or margarine, cut up
Salt
Freshly ground pepper

If the bread dough is refrigerated, bring it back to room temperature.

Preheat the oven to 425 degrees.

Butter the tart mold. Flour your hands and spread the dough in the pan or roll it out. Scatter the butter all over the top, then sprinkle with salt and freshly ground pepper.

Bake on a cookie sheet in the middle of the oven for 10 minutes, or until the top is lightly golden brown. (The cookie sheet is under the pan to catch any butter that might drip over the edges.)

Cut into wedges with a pair of scissors and serve immediately.

Serves 4 to 6

Hay Day's Potato Bread

Three 8-cup loaf pans

1 1/4 pounds russet potatoes
1 tablespoon active dry yeast
1/2 cup granulated sugar
1 cup lukewarm milk
12 tablespoons (1 1/2 sticks) butter, softened
2 large eggs
About 7 cups all-purpose flour
4 teaspoons salt

In a saucepan, cover the potatoes with cold salted water and bring to a boil. Partially cover and cook for 30 minutes, or until tender.

Preheat the oven to 300 degrees and butter the pans.

Drain the potatoes and reserve 1/2 cup potato water. Put the potato water in the freezer for 8 minutes to cool, then sprinkle the yeast and 1 teaspoon sugar over it. Set aside in a warm place for 15 minutes.

Put the potatoes in the oven to dry for 10 minutes. Peel them and mash with an old-fashioned potato masher or ricer or through a strainer. Dice the potato skins into 1/4-inch pieces and fold back into the mashed potatoes.

Put the mashed potatoes in a large bowl and with a wooden spoon slowly beat in the yeast mixture, milk, butter, remaining sugar, and eggs. (This step can be done in a heavy-duty mixer.)

Add salt to the flour and mix. Gradually add 6 cups of flour to the mixture; knead in the last cup by hand.

Cover the dough with a large plastic bag and let rise until doubled. Punch down and knead in an additional 1/3 cup flour. Cut and shape into loaves. Place the dough in the pans, cover with large plastic bags, and set aside until the dough doubles in bulk or comes up to the rims of the pans.

Preheat the oven to 350 degrees.

Bake the loaves for 50 minutes, or until golden brown. Unmold on racks and let cool.

Lucky are the folks who live near the two Hay Day markets in Westport and Greenwich, Connecticut: They can buy this bread fresh from the oven twice a week. It's worth making it at home just for the wonderful aroma emanating from the oven when the bread bakes.

It's a brioche dough with mashed potatoes speckled with the skins of the potatoes. The recipe was created by Mimi Boyd, founder of the original bakery in the Hay Day Westport market. Thanks to my friends Sallie and Alex Van Rensselaer, the owners of Hay Day, we all can make it at home.

For breakfast, I slice the bread 1 inch thick and toast it in the oven on both sides. It's crunchy on the outside and moist inside—delicious.

The difference between this Pennsylvania Dutch bread recipe and Eliza Acton's is that bread flour is used instead of all-purpose flour, and potato water replaces milk. It is a sturdier bread and a little more difficult to knead. The flavor is sensational.

I knead the bread by hand. It takes about 20 minutes to get a soft, smooth dough. In Pennsylvania Dutch kitchens, the bread is kneaded in the evening and left to rise slowly during the night.

Pennsylvania Dutch Potato Bread

Two 8-cup loaf pans

1 1/4 pounds russet potatoes
2 teaspoons active dry yeast
2 tablespoons sugar
4 cups bread flour
1 tablespoon salt

In a saucepan, cover the potatoes with cold salted water and bring to a boil. Partially cover and cook for 30 minutes, or until tender.

Preheat the oven to 300 degrees; butter or oil the loaf pans.

Drain the potatoes and reserve 1/2 cup potato water. Put the potato water in the freezer for 8 minutes to cool. Sprinkle the yeast and 1 teaspoon sugar over the lukewarm water. Set aside in a warm place for 15 minutes.

Put the potatoes to dry in the oven for 10 minutes.

Peel the potatoes and mash them with a potato masher, ricer, or through a strainer, pushing with the back of a large spoon, 1 potato at a time. You should have about 2 1/2 to 3 loosely packed cups mashed potatoes.

In a large bowl, combine the mashed potatoes and the yeast mixture. Mix the flour, salt, and remaining sugar. With a large wooden spoon, gradually mix in the flour. When the dough is too stiff to stir, transfer it to a work surface and knead in the remaining flour, tablespoon by tablespoon. When it becomes difficult to knead because the dough is so elastic, stop kneading for 5 minutes and start over again. Do this several times until *all the flour* is incorporated. (At first, you won't believe that all that flour will be used; keep faith, it will.) Knead the dough until smooth. In all, kneading time is about 20 minutes.

Put the dough in a large bowl, cover with a large plastic bag (a supermarket plastic bag is ideal), and let rise until it doubles in bulk.

Dust flour on the dough and knead it for 1 minute.

Divide the dough in half. Shape each piece into a sausagelike roll to fit in the prepared pans. Once more, cover with a large plastic bag and let rise almost to the tops of the pans (30 minutes in a warm place).

Preheat the oven to 350 degrees.

Bake the loaves in the middle of the preheated oven for 50 minutes, or until the bread is golden brown. Unmold on racks. Cool completely. Wrap in aluminum foil and refrigerate. This bread keeps for several weeks in the refrigerator.

In the French Alps region of Grenoble, where walnuts are a main crop, the bakers make fougasse, *a flat bread with walnuts, brushed with walnut oil.*

When farmers in the region were still baking bread in their bread ovens, it was traditional to keep a piece of dough to make fougasse *after the regular weekly batch of breads was baked. The ovens were still hot enough to bake decorative breads, gratins, and tarts.* Fougasse *was a treat for children, more like cake than the sturdy country bread they were used to.*

Fougasse

- **1 batch Pennsylvania Dutch Potato Bread dough (page 64)**
- **½ cup coarsely chopped walnuts**
- **5 tablespoons walnut oil (if not available, use light olive oil)**

Mix the walnuts with 2 tablespoons walnut oil.

Oil a 17- by 14-inch cookie sheet with some of the remaining walnut oil. Roll out the dough and place it on the oiled cookie sheet, or press the dough and stretch it right on the cookie sheet.

Cut incisions in the dough almost straight through to the cookie sheet, and bury the walnuts in the dough.

With scissors, cut 4-inch-long slits in the dough, to resemble veins in a leaf. Flour your hands and stretch the slits apart as wide as you can so they will not close when the dough rises.

Brush walnut oil over the fougasse. Set aside for 15 minutes.

Preheat the oven to 400 degrees.

Brush the bread once more with walnut oil.

Bake in the middle shelf of the oven until golden brown, about 25 minutes.

Pull apart with fingers and eat the fougasse warm with soup or with cheese.

Serves 8

Potato Focaccia

2 garlic cloves, peeled and cut in slivers
2 tablespoons minced fresh rosemary needles
3 tablespoons olive oil
1 batch Pennsylvania Dutch Potato Bread dough (page 64)

Mix the garlic slivers and rosemary with 2 tablespoons olive oil.

Brush a 12- by 17-inch jellyroll pan with olive oil. Roll out the dough and line the pan with it, or press the dough and stretch it in the pan. With scissors, cut slits all over the surface of the focaccia and bury the rosemary-coated garlic slivers in the slits. Brush more oil over the dough. Set aside for 15 minutes.

Preheat the oven to 350 degrees.

Bake the focaccia on the middle shelf of the oven for 35 minutes. Transfer to a baking rack to cool for a moment or two; serve warm.

Serves 8

I serve this focaccia with soups or as an appetizer garnished with roasted red peppers marinated in olive oil.

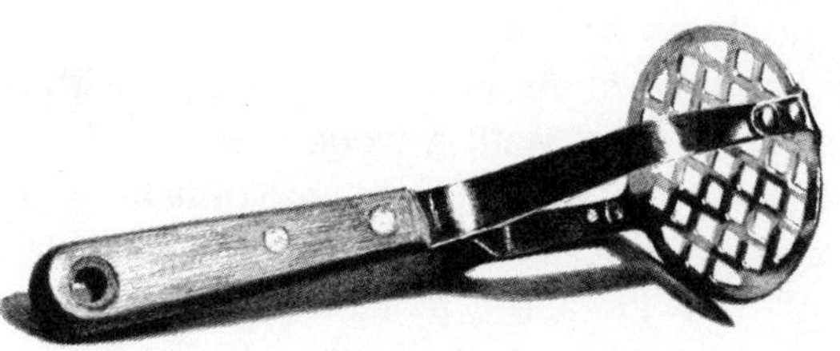

Potato and Pecan Bread

I was inspired to create this recipe by the wholewheat walnut bread of Poilane, the famous bakery in Paris. It is best toasted and served with cheese.

Two 8-cup loaf pans

1¼ pounds russet potatoes
2 teaspoons active dry yeast
1 teaspoon sugar
3½ cups all-purpose flour
½ cup whole wheat flour
1 tablespoon salt
1 cup chopped pecans

In a saucepan, cover the potatoes with cold salted water and bring to a boil. Partially cover and simmer for 30 minutes, or until tender.

Preheat oven to 300 degrees; butter or oil the loaf pans.

Drain the potatoes and reserve 1 cup potato water. Put the potato water in the freezer for 8 minutes to cool to lukewarm, then sprinkle the yeast and sugar over it. Set aside in a warm place for 15 minutes.

Put the potatoes in the oven to dry for 10 minutes.

Peel the potatoes. Mash them with either a potato masher, a ricer, or through a strainer with the back of a spoon, 1 potato at a time. You should have about 2½ to 3 cups mashed potatoes, loosely packed.

Combine the flours and salt.

In a large bowl, combine the yeast mixture with the mashed potatoes and the pecans. With a wooden spoon, incorporate the flours gradually. When the dough gets too difficult to mix, transfer it to a work surface. Knead, gradually adding flour. It takes about 20 minutes of hard kneading to incorporate all of it, but keep faith, it will come together at the end.

Place the dough in a large bowl and cover it with a large plastic bag. When it has doubled in size, sprinkle flour over it and knead in an additional ½ cup flour if the dough is very sticky.

Cut the dough in half. Shape it like two sausages to fit in the prepared pans. Cover with plastic bags and let rise until the dough has once more doubled in bulk, or is almost at the rims of the loaf pans.

Preheat the oven to 400 degrees.

Bake for 45 minutes. Unmold on a cake rack. Well wrapped and refrigerated, the bread will keep for a week or so. It's best eaten warm, soon after it's baked.

Potato and Pecan Rolls

1 batch Potato and Pecan Bread dough
Cornmeal
Oil

When the dough has risen once, punch it down, cover it with a plastic bag, and refrigerate it at least 4 hours or overnight for its second rise.

Flour your hands and knead the dough for a minute. Shape the dough into a circle 8 inches in diameter and cut the circle into 12 wedges. Shape each wedge into a ball the size of a golf ball. Sprinkle with cornmeal and put the rolls to rise on a wooden paddle (a peel). Brush oil over the rolls to prevent drying. Slash the tops with a pair of scissors.

Preheat oven to 400 degrees; put a pizza slab in the oven.

Tip over or loosen the rolls and push them or transfer them with a steel spatula to the hot pizza slab. Bake for about 30 minutes. Transfer them to a baking rack to cool.

Wrapped in plastic bags, the rolls will keep, refrigerated, for several weeks. Reheat them before serving.

NOTE: You can make sourdough bread with the dough. Before shaping the dough into loaves or rolls, set aside 1 cup of dough in a bowl, cover, and refrigerate. When you are ready to make another batch of bread, knead the reserved dough into the new batch of dough you are making, then proceed with the recipe.

Makes 12 4-inch rolls

BREAKFAST BREADS

Croissants are traditionally eaten for breakfast in France, but they make wonderful sandwiches; the blinis are perfect for a Sunday brunch as well as for a light supper. The waffles, doughnuts, and coffee cake are, well, good any time!

Croissants

Yes, you can make croissants with potato bread dough and yes, you can shape them the night before, and yes, you can keep them in the refrigerator.

In one of my cooking demonstrations in a Seattle restaurant, I became very excited because croissants baked in their professional convection oven puffed up much more than in my conventional oven. They were light, and they looked professional, and they tasted very good.

Back in New York, I was ready to demolish half my house to install one of those marvelous ovens, but alas, it got com-

½ pound russet potatoes
¼ cup milk
2 teaspoons active dry yeast
1 tablespoon plus 1 teaspoon sugar
2 cups plus 4 tablespoons all-purpose flour
1 teaspoon salt
12 tablespoons (1½ sticks) unsalted butter, softened

FOR THE GLAZE:

1 tablespoon cream
1 egg white

In a saucepan, cover the potatoes with cold salted water and bring to a boil. Partially cover and simmer for 30 minutes, or until tender.

Preheat the oven to 300 degrees.

Drain the potatoes and reserve ¼ cup of the potato water. Add ¼ cup cold milk to the potato water and sprinkle the yeast and 1 teaspoon sugar over the liquid. Set aside in a warm place for 15 minutes.

Put the potatoes in the oven to dry for 10 minutes.

Peel the potatoes and mash them with a potato masher, ricer, or through a strainer.

Mix 2 cups of flour with the remaining 1 tablespoon sugar and the salt.

In a large bowl, beat the mashed potatoes with the yeast mixture. Gradually beat in the flour, 1 tablespoon at a time. (This step can be done in the bowl of a heavy-duty mixer.) Knead with your hands until the dough is smooth.

Put the soft dough in a 4-quart bowl. Cover with a plastic bag and let rise until doubled in bulk.

Flour your hands and knead the dough for 1 minute with 1 tablespoon flour.

Refrigerate at least 6 hours or overnight.

Knead the soft butter with the remaining 3 tablespoons flour.

Roll out the refrigerated dough into a long 8-inch by 18-inch rectangle. Spread the soft butter mixed with flour over the dough, leaving a ½-inch border, and fold the dough in 3, like a business letter. Turn the dough a quarter way counterclockwise: 12 to 11:45. The dough should look like a book, with the binding on the left. Roll out again to the same size rectangle. Fold again in thirds. Wrap and refrigerate no more than *35 minutes* (otherwise the butter will get too cold).

Roll and fold 4 more times, refrigerating 35 minutes after the second of these folds and after the last fold.

To shape the croissants, roll out the dough into a circle 15 inches in diameter and cut it into 12 wedges. Roll up each wedge, starting from the large base of the triangle.

Put the croissants, point end underneath, on 2 buttered cookie sheets if you are planning to bake them soon; or unprepared cookie sheets if they are to be baked at a later time (see Note below.)

Brush cream over them and let them rise. They should increase by about half their bulk but no more, or they will deflate when baking.

Preheat a convection oven to 350 degrees, a regular oven to 400 degrees.

(continued)

plicated and expensive. So expensive in fact, that I would have had to make croissants every day of my life to pay back the investment. Instead, I bought a table model convection oven, which turned out to work very well. Because of the size, I can bake only 6 croissants at a time, but it's worth it.

Professional bakers have controlled temperature and humidity boxes in which they let the croissant dough rise. This is impossible at home, but I have devised a timing system using the refrigerator, and it works.

Croissants are made of soft bread dough layered with butter and folded several times like puff pastry. The dough must be refrigerated between folds to firm up the butter just enough to make it easy to roll out the dough for the next fold. If the butter gets too hard, it develops unattractive small lumps in the dough. In addition, when the dough is finally shaped into croissants, the hard butter tends to come through the dough, and immediately melts in the oven before the croissants have time to bake, making a mess. So it's a question of timing the dough in the refrigerator.

Brush egg white glaze over the croissants. Bake for 10 to 15 minutes, or until puffy and golden brown. Serve warm.

NOTE: To hold for later baking, cover the croissants with a large plastic bag and put the cookie sheet in the refrigerator. The timing in the refrigerator is not important after the croissants are shaped. The butter must come to room temperature for the last rise, but there is no more rolling—the action that breaks up the cold butter.

Remove the croissants from the refrigerator 1 to 3 hours before baking and transfer them to 2 buttered cookie sheets. When the weather is warm and humid, the croissants will rise faster than in cold weather.

Makes 12 croissants

I spent a week in the kitchens of Taillevent, the best known French restaurant in the world. I fell in love with Chef Deligne's blinis, along with the little skillets in which he cooked them. They are 4 inches in diameter and made of heavy steel. You don't need to run to Paris to buy blini skillets, but if you get the urge, buy them at Dehillerin, 18–20 rue Coquilliere, Paris 1.

Don't confuse blinis with blintzes; the former is a yeasty pancake, the latter is a crêpe. Oat flour or buckwheat flour is

Taillevent's Blinis

1/4 pound russet potatoes
3/4 cup milk
4 tablespoons butter or margarine, softened
2 teaspoons active dry yeast
2 teaspoons sugar
1 cup all-purpose flour
1/4 cup oat or buckwheat flour
1 teaspoon salt
2 egg yolks

In a saucepan, cover the potatoes with cold salted water and bring to a boil. Partially cover and simmer for 30 minutes, or until tender.

Scald the milk. Turn off the heat and stir in the butter. Set aside.

Preheat the oven to 300 degrees.

Drain the potatoes, reserving 1/2 cup of potato water. Put the potato water in the freezer for 8 minutes to cool and sprinkle the yeast and sugar over the water. Set aside in a warm place for 15 minutes.

Put the potatoes in the oven to dry for 10 minutes.

Peel the potatoes and mash them with a potato masher, ricer, or through a strainer. You should have about 1 cup of mashed potatoes, lightly packed.

Mix the flours, mashed potatoes, and salt together.

In a large bowl, combine the yeast mixture and the egg yolks; stir. Gradually incorporate the mixture of flours and mashed potatoes, alternating with the milk-butter mixture. (This step can be done in a heavy-duty mixer.)

Cover and let stand 40 minutes to rise.

Brush melted butter in a 10-inch nonstick skillet. Use 1/8 cup batter to make 3-inch blinis in the skillet. Cook for 2 minutes on each side. Transfer the blinis to a preheated platter, brush melted butter on each one while still hot, and continue making blinis with the remaining batter. (I make blinis in several skillets to speed up the cooking.)

Serve the blinis with maple syrup or jam for breakfast, or offer them as an appetizer with smoked salmon or sour cream and salmon caviar (see page 6).

Makes about 16 3-inch blinis, serving 8

part of the traditional blini batter. Health food stores carry both flours. I prefer oat to buckwheat, but it is a matter of taste.

Scrambled eggs and blinis with maple syrup make a great breakfast! At Taillevent, the blinis are served as an appetizer with smoked salmon.

My husband's Aunt Laura never wanted me to have this recipe, for fear I would become very rich publishing it. I don't blame her; she worked hard trying to reproduce the shshky Uncle Tony ate as a child in Bohemia. Then one day, after criticizing every batch she made, he said yes, the shshky were just like his mother made them. What a relief for Laura!

Shshky

BOHEMIAN POTATO DOUGHNUTS

½ pound russet potatoes
1⅔ cups milk
8 tablespoons (1 stick) unsalted butter
1 tablespoon active dry yeast
3 tablespoons plus 1 teaspoon sugar
4 cups all-purpose flour
1 teaspoon salt
1 teaspoon grated lemon peel
3 cups corn oil
1 cup sugar

In a saucepan, cover the potatoes with cold salted water and bring to a boil. Partially cover and simmer for 20 minutes, or until tender.

Scald the milk and, off the heat, stir in the butter. Set aside to cool.

Preheat the oven to 300 degrees.

Drain the potatoes and reserve ¼ cup potato water. Put the water in the freezer for 8 minutes to cool. Sprinkle the yeast and 1 teaspoon of sugar over the lukewarm potato water. Set aside in a warm place for 15 minutes.

Put the potatoes in the oven to dry for 10 minutes.

Peel and mash the potatoes either with a potato masher, ricer, or through a strainer, 1 potato at a time. You should have about 1 loosely packed cup of mashed potatoes.

In a large bowl, mix the mashed potatoes with the yeast mixture and the milk-butter mixture.

Mix the flour, 3 tablespoons sugar, salt, and lemon peel. In a heavy-duty mixer with the paddle attachment, or by hand with a wooden spoon, start incorporating the flour into the mashed potato mixture, ¼ cup at a time. Flour your hands and knead until the dough is elastic and soft.

Put the dough in a large greased bowl. Cover with a large plastic bag and let rise until doubled.

Cut the dough into 4 pieces. On a lightly floured board, roll 1 piece of dough at a time to a circle ½ inch thick and 10 inches in diameter. Stamp out 3½-inch doughnuts with a cookie cutter or with the top of a glass. Tear a hole in the middle of each doughnut with your index finger and stretch it ¼ inch wide. Roll out the scraps and make more doughnuts.

Place the doughnuts on greased pans. Let them rise in a warm place just until they feel spongy and light, about 15 minutes. Don't let them overrise or they will deflate when they are fried. Make as many doughnuts as you want, refrigerating the remaining dough. It lasts several days in the refrigerator.

Heat the oil to 300 degrees in a deep-fryer or in a deep skillet, making sure the oil comes only ⅓ of the way up the sides of the pan. Turn each doughnut upside down and lower several of them into the hot fat; they'll continue to rise while frying. Deep-fry until golden brown, 1 to 2 minutes on each side, turning the doughnuts with a fork.

Transfer them to a rack and coat with granulated sugar while still warm. They are best eaten warm.

Makes 30 doughnuts

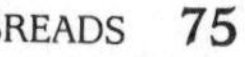

Belgium is renowned for its yeast waffles. Just before baking, beaten egg whites are folded into the batter to create light-as-feather waffles. I serve them for a late breakfast or brunch with berries and sour cream in the summer and with maple syrup in the winter.

Potato Waffles

½ pound russet potatoes
2 teaspoons active dry yeast
2 tablespoons plus 1 teaspoon sugar
1 cup all-purpose flour
¼ teaspoon salt
2 eggs, separated
1 cup milk
4 tablespoons (½ stick) unsalted butter, softened
Confectioners' sugar

In a saucepan, cover the potatoes with cold salted water and bring to a boil. Partially cover and simmer for 30 minutes, or until tender.

Preheat the oven to 300 degrees.

Drain the potatoes and reserve ½ cup of the potato water. Put the potato water in the freezer for 8 minutes to cool, then sprinkle the yeast and 1 teaspoon sugar over it. Set aside in a warm place for 15 minutes.

Put the potatoes in the oven to dry for 10 minutes.

Peel and mash the potatoes with a potato masher, ricer or through a strainer. You should have about 1 loosely packed cup of mashed potatoes.

In a large bowl combine the flour, the remaining 2 tablespoons sugar, and salt.

Mix the mashed potatoes with the yeast mixture, egg yolks, milk, and butter (can be done in a heavy-duty mixer or by hand).

Whisk all the ingredients until smooth. Cover with a large plastic bag and set aside to rise for 1 hour.

Beat the egg whites until firm. With a wooden spoon, gently deflate the batter, add the flour, and fold in the egg whites.

Heat a waffle iron. On a 7-inch-diameter waffle iron, spread about ⅔ cup batter; the layer of batter should be about ⅛ inch thick. (Adjust the amount of batter for a larger or smaller iron.) Cook until all the steam is evaporated, about 5 minutes.

When all the waffles are cooked, sprinkle with confectioners' sugar.

Makes four 7-inch waffles

Variation

If you don't have a waffle iron, make pancakes instead of waffles. Brush oil and heat a nonstick skillet. Pour a scant ½ cup batter, tilt the skillet spreading the batter to a 5-inch pancake. When the bottom of the pancake is golden brown (about 3–4 minutes), flip it over and cook for 2–3 more minutes or until golden brown. Makes 6 pancakes. Serve with maple syrup or honey.

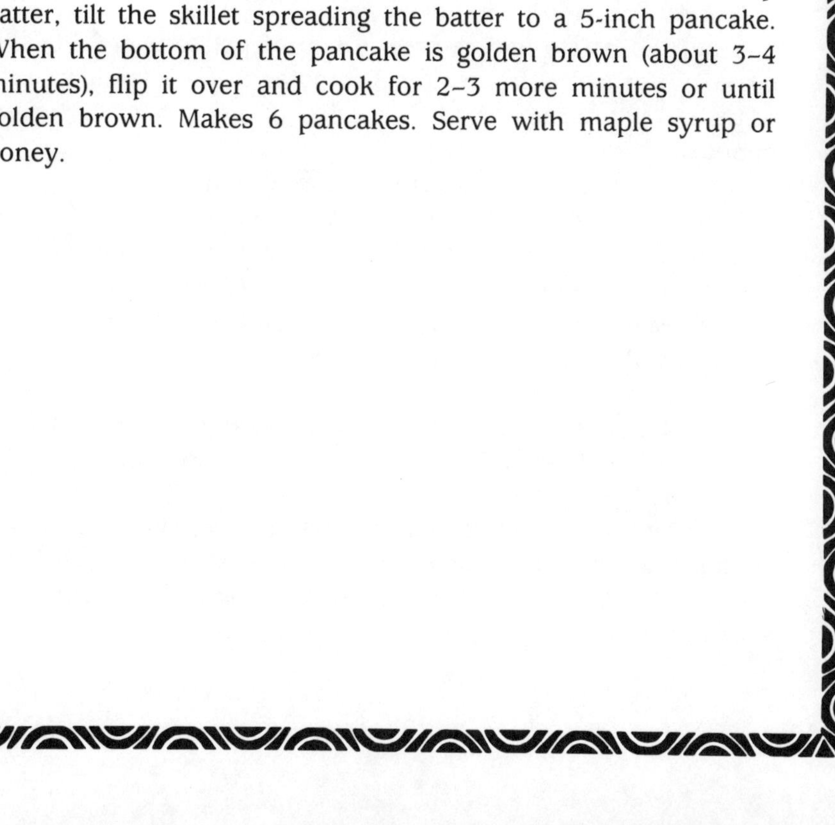

Potato Coffee Cake

"Allow the dough to rise overnight in a large, white dishpan lined with wax paper and covered with a red sweater," says Mrs. Anna Fuchs, from Westerville, Ohio, who makes this marvelous potato coffee cake. I hope Mrs. Fuchs will forgive me for not knitting a red sweater for her cake, nor do I have a white dishpan. Instead, I let it rise in a blue bowl, covered, alas, with a supermarket plastic bag! But the plastic creates the warmth needed for the cake to rise just as well as a red sweater.

Two 8-cup loaf pans

1/3 pound russet potato
1/2 cup plus 1 teaspoon sugar
1 tablespoon active dry yeast
1/4 cup vegetable shortening
5 to 6 cups all-purpose flour
1 cup milk, scalded
8 tablespoons (1 stick) unsalted butter
1/4 teaspoon baking powder
1/2 tablespoon salt
1 egg, lightly beaten
1 tablespoon heavy cream
1/2 cup brown sugar

In a saucepan, cover the potato with cold salted water. Bring to a boil, partially cover, and simmer for 20 minutes, or until tender.

Preheat the oven to 300 degrees.

Drain the potato and reserve 1/2 cup of potato water. Put the potato water in the freezer for 8 minutes to cool; sprinkle with yeast and 1 teaspoon sugar. Set aside in a warm place for 15 minutes.

Put the potato in the oven to dry for 10 minutes.

Peel and mash the potato with a potato masher, a ricer, or through a strainer. You should have about 1 cup mashed potato.

Combine the remaining 1/2 cup sugar and the shortening.

In a heavy-duty mixer fitted with the paddle attachment, or in a large bowl with a wooden spoon, beat the mashed potato, the yeast mixture, and the shortening and sugar mixture with 1 cup of flour. Cover with a large plastic bag and let rise for 1 hour.

Scald the milk and add the butter. Set aside to cool.

Add the baking powder and salt to the remaining flour.

Beat the egg and milk-butter mixture into the potato batter and gradually add the flour. When the batter turns into a dough and is too stiff to beat with a wooden spoon, or in the electric mixer, knead the remaining flour into the dough with your hands, 1/4 cup of flour at a time. Knead until very smooth. Cover with a large plastic bag and let rise overnight.

Punch down and knead the dough for 1 minute or so. Cut the dough in half. Shape each half into a large sausage-shaped roll to fit in the buttered pans.

Brush cream over the loaves. Cut diagonal gashes in the dough and press brown sugar in with your fingers. Sprinkle 1/3 cup brown sugar over the surface of each cake.

Cover the loaves with large plastic bags and let rise until they reach the top of the pans, about 2 hours in winter, less during the summer.

Preheat the oven to 350 degrees.

Bake for 40 minutes or until golden brown. Serve warm. Well wrapped, the coffee cake will keep several weeks in the refrigerator. Slice, butter, and toast one side.

5.
Main Courses

Think of the potato as a vegetable and not as a starch. Eating potatoes every day is nutritious and delicious; move the potato from the wings as a side dish and give it center stage.

In this chapter of main dishes, baking, all-purpose, and new potatoes are part of the repertory in which the potato has a starring role.

Arabian Pork Chops

Lucille Schauer, my cooking connection in Sun City, Arizona, gave me this recipe, which she learned to make in Wisconsin. The title must be ironic, since Muslims do not eat pork. This is very simple to make and very good to eat.

2 tablespoons olive oil
2 pork chops, 3/4 inch thick
1 teaspoon salt
Freshly ground pepper
1 onion, peeled and sliced 1/8 inch thick
1 large tomato, sliced 1/4 inch thick
1 large russet, Yukon Gold, White Rose, or Red Nordland potato, peeled and sliced 1/8 inch to 1/16 inch thick

Preheat the oven to 325 degrees.

Heat the oil in a 10-inch skillet and brown the chops for several minutes on each side.

Transfer the chops to a 10-inch square baking dish. Add 1 cup water to the skillet. Bring to a boil, scraping the bottom of the pan to dissolve the drippings. Boil down to 1/2 cup. Set aside.

Season the chops with salt and pepper. Top with slices of onion and tomato. Overlap the potato slices on top, add salt and pepper, and pour over the reserved liquid.

Cover the pan and bake in the center of the oven for 2 hours.

Set the broiler on high, uncover the dish, and broil for about 1 minute to add color to the potatoes. Serve immediately.

Serves 2

Country Pork Roast with Roasted Potatoes

½ teaspoon dried thyme
2 teaspoons salt
1 garlic clove, peeled and cut into slivers
3 pounds butt-end pork roast
1 teaspoon oil
1 tablespoon Dijon mustard
1½ pounds Yukon Gold, Red Nordland, White Rose, or russet potatoes, peeled and diced into 1-inch cubes (4½ cups)

As a child, I spent many happy summers at a farm near Poitiers, in western France, where the lady of the house made this delicious pork roast with potatoes.

Combine the thyme and 1 teaspoon salt and dip the slivers of garlic in the mixture. Make incisions in the pork and bury the garlic in the meat.

Rub about 1 teaspoon oil all over the meat. Place the pork roast in the broiler pan of your oven. (It can be prepared to this point the day before roasting; keep refrigerated.)

Preheat the oven to 400 degrees.

Put the pork roast in the center of the oven and roast for 45 minutes.

Remove the roast from the oven and brush it with mustard. Scatter the potatoes around the meat and sprinkle with the remaining 1 teaspoon salt. Stir the potatoes around the roast. Pour over 1 cup water. Roast for another hour, stirring the potatoes once in a while to brown evenly.

Set the roast aside for 10 minutes before slicing.

Serves 4

Roasted Chicken on a Bed of Potato Straw Mats

My favorite bistro dinner is a simple roasted chicken served on a bed of very thin and crusty potato straw mats. It is easy to prepare and not too time-consuming. Start the meal with soup and serve cheese and fruit for dessert; it's a feast, and it's cheap too!

You may want to serve 2 potato mats per person; in that case, double the amount of potatoes given in the recipe. Preparation will go faster if you use several skillets.

***For the potato mats:** 1 nonstick skillet 6 inches wide at the top, or a crêpe pan*

One 3-pound roasting chicken
1 tablespoon chicken, goose, or duck fat, or oil
1 pound Yukon Gold, Red Nordland, Pontiac, White Rose, or russet potatoes, grated through the medium blade of a mouli-julienne, food processor, or the coarse side of a hand grater (4 cups)
2 tablespoons clarified butter or margarine
Salt
Freshly ground pepper
3 tablespoons butter or margarine
4 cups watercress, stems removed

Preheat the oven to 400 degrees.

Brush the chicken all over with fat. Place in a roasting pan, just the size of the chicken (a black iron skillet is perfect), breast side up.

Roast the chicken in the middle shelf of the oven for 1 hour and 15 minutes. Baste it occasionally with the rendered fat.

Plunge the grated potatoes in a large pan of cold water. Drain and rinse once more. Pat very dry.

Pour 1 teaspoon clarified butter or margarine in a nonstick skillet or crêpe pan. When the fat is hot, swirl it around the bottom of the skillet, add 1 cup grated potatoes, and pack down the straggly ends of the potatoes with a cake turner, smoothing out the surface. Sprinkle with salt and freshly ground pepper and place 2 teaspoons of small wedges of butter or margarine around the sides of the potato mat. Cover the skillet with a lid and cook on medium heat for 10 minutes.

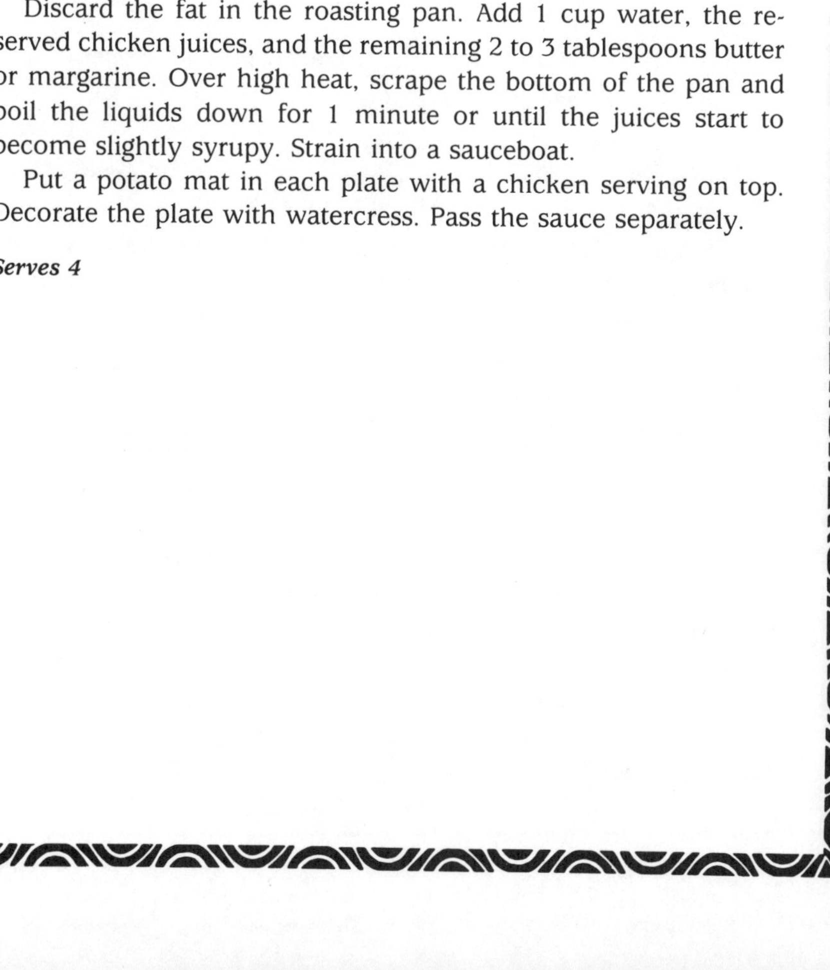

Lift the lid twice during that time, lifting it straight up to avoid steam falling back into the potatoes; dry the underside of the lid.

After 10 minutes, check the underside; when crisp and golden, invert the potato mat onto a plate.

Add a bit more clarified butter or margarine to the skillet and when the fat sizzles, slide the potato mat back into the pan. Cook uncovered for about 5 minutes, or until the underside is crisp and golden. Reserve, and repeat with the next 3 straw mats. (If you make larger straw mats—in a 10-inch skillet for instance—put in 2 cups of grated potatoes and cook 15 to 20 minutes on 1 side and about 10 minutes on the other side.)

Carve the chicken into several pieces, reserving the juices that accumulate.

Discard the fat in the roasting pan. Add 1 cup water, the reserved chicken juices, and the remaining 2 to 3 tablespoons butter or margarine. Over high heat, scrape the bottom of the pan and boil the liquids down for 1 minute or until the juices start to become slightly syrupy. Strain into a sauceboat.

Put a potato mat in each plate with a chicken serving on top. Decorate the plate with watercress. Pass the sauce separately.

Serves 4

Chicken Fricassee with Fatless Mashed Potatoes

In many French farm households, mashed potatoes are seasoned with the water in which the potatoes have boiled, without any milk, butter, or oil, and they still taste very good. Topped with a simple fricassee of chicken, the dish is delectable.

FOR THE FRICASSEE:

2 pounds of chicken wings, legs, and thighs, cleaved into 2-inch pieces
Flour for dredging
3 tablespoons olive oil
Salt and freshly ground pepper
2 large tomatoes in season, chopped (2 cups), or 1 pint cherry tomatoes, chopped (2 cups)
2 large garlic cloves, peeled and cut into slivers
2 scallions, thinly sliced

FOR THE POTATOES:

2 pounds russet potatoes
1½ teaspoons salt
Freshly ground pepper

Dredge the chicken pieces in flour, shaking off excess. In a large skillet, heat the olive oil. Brown half the chicken until golden brown (about 15 minutes); season with salt and freshly ground pepper. Set aside and repeat with the second batch of chicken, adding more oil if necessary.

Meanwhile, toss together the tomatoes, garlic, and scallions, season with salt and pepper, and set aside.

Put all the chicken back into the skillet and sprinkle the garlic, tomatoes, and scallion mixture on top and stir-fry for 1 minute or so. Cover and simmer over medium heat for 15 more minutes. Serve on top of the fatless mashed potatoes.

In a large pan, cover the potatoes with cold salted water and bring to a boil. Partially cover and cook for 30 minutes, or until the potatoes are tender. Drain and reserve the potato water.

Peel the potatoes and mash them with a potato masher, ricer, or through a strainer, 1 potato at a time.

Reheat the mashed potatoes and moisten with potato water

until they reach the desired thickness. Season with the salt and lots of freshly ground pepper. Serve with the chicken fricassee.

Serves 4

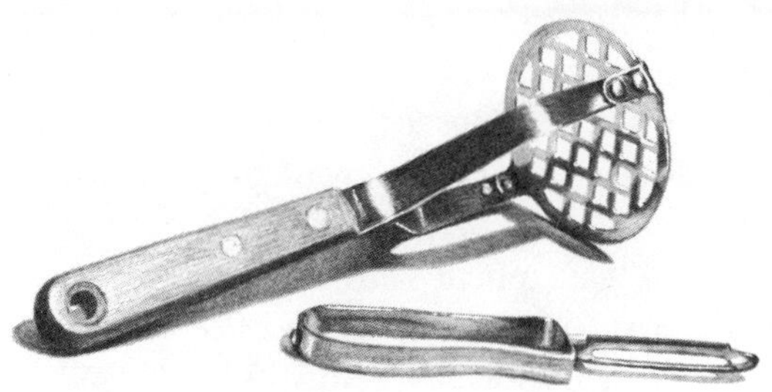

Chicken Pot Pie with Potato Gnocchi

- ½ recipe Italian Gnocchi (page 187)
- 2 tablespoons butter or margarine, melted
- 2 tablespoons corn oil
- 1½ pounds chicken parts, cleaved into 2-inch pieces
- ½ pound breakfast sausages, cut into 1-inch slices
- 1 medium onion, peeled and thinly sliced
- ¼ pound mushrooms, quartered
- ¼ cup green olives
- Salt and freshly ground pepper
- 1 sprig fresh tarragon, or 1 teaspoon dried tarragon
- 4 phyllo pastry leaves
- ½ cup chicken stock or heavy cream

The amounts of gnocchi and chicken noted are only guidelines. This is a flexible recipe where you can add or subtract without ruining the dish. I cook it in a deep Pyrex dish for my family, but I also serve it for dinner parties in individual ovenproof soup bowls.

First, prepare the potato gnocchi; when they are poached, transfer them to a 3-quart Pyrex casserole with 1 tablespoon melted butter.

In a large skillet, heat the oil and brown the chicken pieces until golden brown, about 15 minutes. Add them to the gnocchi.

Brown the sausages for 5 minutes and add them to the gnocchi. Don't wash the skillet; set it aside.

(continued)

Sauté the onion for 3 minutes; add to the gnocchi.

Sauté the mushrooms for 3 minutes with the olives, adding more oil if necessary. Add them to the gnocchi.

Season with salt and freshly ground pepper and add the sprig of fresh tarragon or season with the dried tarragon.

Preheat the oven to 350 degrees.

Unroll 4 phyllo pastry leaves in front of you; brush butter on the first leaf and, with the buttered side down, cover the baking dish with the phyllo leaf; repeat with the next 3 leaves, each buttered side down. Trim the phyllo around the dish, leaving about 1 inch overhang all around; seal the phyllo leaves to the pan. Brush the remaining melted butter on top of the dough and bake the casserole in the center of the preheated oven for 30 minutes, or until the pastry is golden brown.

Reheat the skillet, pour in the chicken stock or cream. Bring to a boil, scraping the bottom of the skillet. Boil for 1 minute, and strain.

To serve, cut the pastry in 4 wedges, set aside; serve the chicken and gnocchi in the center of each plate, ladle 1 tablespoon of sauce over it, then cover with the pastry.

Serves 4

Irish Stew

- 5 pounds lamb stew meat (neck or shoulder), trimmed of all fat and cut into 2-inch cubes
- 2 leeks, tough green parts removed
- 1 tablespoon salt
- 1 pound Yukon Gold, Red La Rouge, or White Rose potatoes, quartered and unpeeled
- ½ pound pearl onions
- ½ cup cherry tomatoes
- 4 tablespoons (½ stick) butter
- ¼ cup flour
- ¼ cup minced fresh parsley

I serve Irish stew like a soup. It's a very simple peasant dish that benefits from reheating. I serve it with Eliza Acton's Potato Bread (page 60) and I always make a fruit tart for dessert.

In a large dutch oven or stockpot, cover the meat with cold salted water. Bring to a boil and skim off the scum. Drain the meat and wash each piece under cold running water to remove any scum left on the meat.

Put the meat back in the pot. Cover with 4 cups of water, or enough to barely cover the meat. Add the leeks and 2 teaspoons salt. Bring to a boil, cover tightly, and simmer for 1½ hours.

Place the potatoes, onions, and tomatoes on top of the leeks. Sprinkle on the remaining 1 teaspoon salt. Cover the pot and steam for ½ hour, or until tender.

With a skimmer, transfer the meat and vegetables to a soup tureen and keep warm.

Mash the butter and flour together. Bring the liquid back to a boil and whisk in the butter mixture to thicken it. Simmer for 10 minutes. Pour over the meat and vegetables.

Ladle the stew into soup bowls and sprinkle minced parsley on top.

Serves 6

Cotelettes Champvallon is quintessential good home cooking. It is easy to make, and out of the most banal ingredients comes a delicious dish with an unusual and very appetizing presentation.

This is one of many regional dishes in which the baking pot is important for success. I use a 3-quart Pyrex casserole with a glass cover. I can check on the potatoes while they cook. They take on a splendid golden color, with slightly crispy tops and bottoms. The meat is fork-tender, melting in with the potatoes and the aromatic vegetables.

Fricassee of Potatoes and Lamb Chops

1 rack of lamb cut into 8 rib lamb chops, the rib ends cut 2½ inches above the loin
¼ cup oil
Flour for dredging
3 medium onions, peeled and chopped (1½ cups)
3 carrots, peeled and chopped (2 cups)
1½ teaspoons salt
Freshly ground pepper
2 tablespoons flour
1½ pounds russet, Yukon Gold, Red Nordland, or White Rose potatoes, peeled and sliced ⅛ inch and 1/16 inch thick

Preheat the oven to 350 degrees.

Remove the double thickness of fat interlaced with a thin layer of meat from the chops, if it has not been done by the butcher. Discard the fat from the rib ends and strip them to the bone. (This technique is called frenching the chops.)

In a large skillet, heat 3 tablespoons of the oil. Dredge half the chops in flour, shake off the excess, and brown them in the hot fat, 3 minutes on each side. Transfer to a plate and brown the remaining chops.

Lower the heat and add the onions and carrots to the skillet. Cook for 10 minutes, until the onions are soft but not brown. Season with ½ teaspoon of the salt and freshly ground pepper. Transfer to a plate and reserve.

In the same skillet, heat the remaining 1 tablespoon oil. Sprinkle in the flour and whisk it into the oil. When smooth, add 2 cups water. Cook for 10 minutes to thicken to the consistency of light cream. Set aside.

Put half the onions and carrots at the bottom of a 3-quart casserole. Nestle the chops vertically in the vegetable mixture, with the rib ends standing up against the sides but not sticking out of the pan. Add the remaining onions and carrots between the chops and in the center.

Rinse the potato slices in cold water but do not pat dry. Season the potatoes with the remaining 1 teaspoon salt and freshly ground pepper. Overlap the potato slices on top of the onions, carrots, and meat, but leave the chop rib ends sticking out.

Pour the sauce over the potatoes. Cover tightly and bake for 2 hours in the center of the oven, or until the potatoes are golden brown. Serve immediately.

Serves 4

Scalloped Potatoes à la Boulangère with a Leg of Lamb

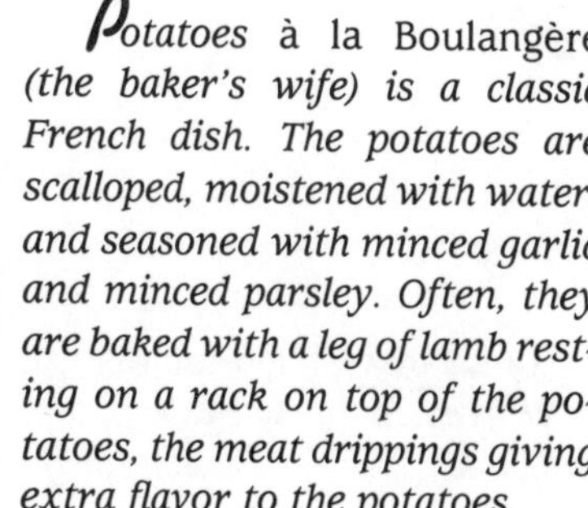

Potatoes à la Boulangère (the baker's wife) is a classic French dish. The potatoes are scalloped, moistened with water, and seasoned with minced garlic and minced parsley. Often, they are baked with a leg of lamb resting on a rack on top of the potatoes, the meat drippings giving extra flavor to the potatoes.

One 4-pound leg of lamb, shank end, all fat removed
1 garlic clove, peeled and cut into 6 slivers
1 teaspoon fresh rosemary, minced
3 pounds Yukon Gold, Red Nordland, or White Rose potatoes, peeled and sliced between 1/8 inch and 1/16 inch thick (8 cups)
4 garlic cloves, peeled and minced
1/3 cup minced parsley
2 teaspoons salt
Freshly ground pepper
2 tablespoons olive oil

Preheat the oven to 450 degrees.

Make deep incisions in the leg of lamb and in them bury the slivers of garlic and the minced rosemary.

(continued)

Toss the potato slices, minced garlic, and parsley together; season with 1½ teaspoons of the salt and freshly ground pepper. Overlap the potatoes in the bottom of an oiled 3-quart baking dish. Pour 1½ cups water over them and dribble on 1 tablespoon of the olive oil.

Place a rack in the baking dish on top of the potatoes and place the leg of lamb on it. Brush the remaining 1 tablespoon olive oil over the lamb and sprinkle with salt and pepper.

Roast for 20 minutes at 450 degrees. Lower the temperature to 400 degrees and continue roasting for 45 minutes more for medium-rare lamb or 1 hour for well-done lamb. Transfer the lamb to a carving board. Cover it with aluminum foil and let stand 15 minutes. Check the potatoes; if they need to cook a little longer, leave them in the oven.

Slice the lamb and reheat the juices that spewed out of it. Serve with the potatoes.

Serves 6

Reuchtis with Veal Stroganoff

Geschnetzeltes reuchtis *is a veal stroganoff with a potato pancake. This cooking originates with the mountain people of Switzerland and not with the chefs in the international palaces for which Switzerland is so famous. The food is plain, perhaps a little heavy, but it has*

1½ pounds Yukon Gold, Red Pontiac, or White Rose potatoes
4 tablespoons (½ stick) unsalted butter or margarine
1 pound boned veal shoulder, cut 2 inches long, 1 inch wide, and ¼ inch thick
1 medium onion, peeled and thinly sliced
1½ teaspoons salt
Freshly ground pepper
3 tablespoons corn oil or lard
1 teaspoon flour (optional)
¼ cup heavy cream or plain yogurt (optional)

Several hours ahead of time, cover the potatoes with a large amount of cold salted water. Bring to a boil, cover, and cook for 35 minutes, or until tender.

Drain the potatoes but do not peel them. Set aside until cold.

For the meat, melt the butter or margarine in a large skillet. Add the meat and cook over high heat, until all the water spews out of the meat and starts to evaporate, about 5 minutes.

Stir in the onion and cook over medium heat until the meat and the onion change to a light amber color. Season with half the salt and freshly ground pepper. Transfer the meat and onion to a strainer placed on top of a bowl to drain the extra butter, and set aside while preparing the *reuchtis*. Save the drained butter.

Peel the cold potatoes and slice them between 1/8 inch and 1/16 inch thick. Heat 3 tablespoons oil or lard in a 10-inch nonstick skillet. When the fat is hot, add the potato slices and stir-fry for about 1 minute. Season with the remaining salt and freshly ground pepper. Continue cooking over medium heat for another 10 minutes to brown as many slices of potatoes as possible; don't worry if not all the slices are browned.

With the back of a cake turner, push down on the potatoes, but do not mash them into a purée. Cook about 15 minutes more or until the bottom side of the pancake is crispy. Shake the skillet to loosen the bottom of the cake and invert it on a serving dish. Set aside in a warm place while finishing the veal stroganoff.

Reheat the veal and onion over medium heat with 1 tablespoon of the drained butter or margarine. If you wish, combine the flour and cream, pour the mixture over the meat, and stir-fry until the cream coats the meat. Taste for seasoning.

Serve the *reuchtis* with the meat on the side.

Serves 4

lots of taste. The Swiss drink café au lait with most of their meals, horrifying their French and Italian neighbors who prefer a cold dry white wine with the reuchtis *and veal.*

Poached Fish with an Herb Sauce and Steamed Potatoes

When I eat fish, I think I have done a good deed and I feel virtuous. I learned to prepare fish under duress. In my childhood, my mother made me eat fish to become smart; today, my doctor wants me to eat fish to stay healthy. Dutifully, I prepare fish. My students clamor for it because they know I will not prepare something that is not tasty. For me, food is taste; I am not like Molière's miser, who had engraved on his mantel: "We eat to live and not live to eat."

Poaching is my favorite way to prepare fish, but the fish must be very fresh. Fresh fish will have clear eyes; the longer it stays on ice, the more opaque the eyes become and the less fresh it smells.

I dedicate this recipe to my lovely internist, Edith Langner, who wants all her patients to eat fish! (When I am bad, I skip the fish. I steam the potatoes and eat them with this herb sauce.)

2 sprigs fresh tarragon
1 onion, unpeeled
1 tablespoon salt
2¼ pounds fish (salmon, cod, halibut, or sturgeon—not tuna), about 3 inches thick and 6 inches long
2 pounds small Red La Rouge or La Soda, small Yukon Gold, Yellow Finnish, or Ruby Crescent potatoes

FOR THE GREEN SAUCE:

1 cooked egg yolk
1 teaspoon Dijon mustard
2 garlic cloves, peeled and mashed
2 tablespoons each minced parsley, tarragon, and chives
¼ cup watercress leaves, minced
1 tablespoon capers, minced
2 tablespoons wine vinegar
½ cup olive oil
Salt
Freshly ground pepper

FOR THE PRESENTATION:

1 red pepper
1 head Bibb lettuce
Black olives

In a large pan, bring 2 quarts of water to a boil with the tarragon, onion, and salt. Turn the heat down and add the fish. Cover tightly and simmer with the water just quivering for 15 minutes. Remove the fish and drain on a rack or in a strainer. Skin the fish and cut it into ½-inch cubes.

Pour about 1 inch of water into the bottom of a large pan and bring to a boil. Fit the steamer into the boiling water, put in the potatoes, cover, and steam for 15 to 20 minutes, depending on the size and varieties of the potatoes.

Meanwhile, prepare the herb sauce: In the bowl of a food processor, combine the egg yolk, mustard, garlic, herbs, watercress, and capers. With the motor running, pour the vinegar through the chute, then gradually dribble in the oil. Stop and scrape the sides of the bowl and process once more for another 10 seconds. Season with salt and pepper to taste, and add more herbs to taste. (This can also be done in a blender.)

Char the pepper on a burner, turning it occasionally to broil it evenly. Put in a sturdy plastic bag to cool.

Peel the pepper, remove the seeds, and cut it into strips 1/8 inch wide.

For the presentation: Line a large serving dish with Bibb lettuce leaves. Place fish and potatoes on individual lettuce leaves, garnishing the top with strips of pepper. Scatter black olives on the platter and pass a sauceboat with the herb sauce.

Serves 8 as a first course, 4 as a main course

Pisto Manchego

SPANISH RATATOUILLE WITH ROASTED POTATOES

Pisto Manchego *originates in the Mancha region of Spain. My friend Viviana Carballo brought this recipe back from Madrid. It's a tasty sautéed vegetable dish with bacon and ham, great for family dinners. It's also very good without bacon and ham: Just substitute olive oil for the fat and add more spices to replace the meat, putting in hot peppers to heighten the flavors.*

3/4 pound slab bacon, cut into 1/2-inch cubes (2 cups)
1/2 pound boiled ham, cut into 1/2-inch cubes (2 cups)
2 onions, peeled and thinly sliced (2 cups)
1 green bell pepper, cut into strips 1/8-inch wide (1 1/2 cups)
1 red bell pepper, cut into strips 1/8-inch wide (1 1/2 cups)
5 large garlic cloves, peeled and minced (2 tablespoons)
1 1/2 teaspoons salt
Freshly ground pepper
1 pound tomatoes, seeded and cut into 1-inch cubes (2 cups), or 1 pint cherry tomatoes, halved
3 small zucchini, cut into 1/2-inch cubes (2 cups)
1/4 teaspoon paprika
1/2 teaspoon dried oregano
1/4 teaspoon dried thyme
2 pounds White Rose, Yukon Gold, or Red Nordland potatoes, peeled and cut into 1/2-inch cubes (6 cups)
1/4 cup olive oil

In a large skillet, cook the bacon for 10 minutes, or until crisp. With a slotted spoon, transfer it to a bowl and set aside.

Sauté the ham for 5 minutes in the bacon fat. Transfer to the bowl with the bacon.

Drain off the bacon fat. Spoon out 3 tablespoons bacon fat and pour it back into the skillet. Sauté the onions, peppers, and garlic for 5 minutes over medium heat, being careful not to burn them. Sprinkle with 1 teaspoon salt and freshly ground pepper. Cover and simmer for 10 minutes.

Add the tomatoes and zucchini with the paprika and herbs and cook the mixture for 15 minutes, uncovered, stirring occasionally.

Stir in the bacon and ham and cook for another 5 minutes.

In a saucepan, cover the potatoes with cold salted water and bring to a boil. Turn off the heat, drain, and divide the potatoes into 2 batches.

Heat 2 tablespoons olive oil in each of two 10-inch nonstick skillets. Sauté the potatoes over medium high heat for 10 minutes, until lightly browned on all sides, stirring occasionally. Sprinkle with ½ teaspoon salt and freshly ground pepper; cover the skillet, lower the heat, and cook for 5 minutes.

Uncover, raise the heat, and stir-fry the potatoes for another 2 to 3 minutes, or until golden brown.

Reheat the vegetables and serve with the roasted potatoes.

Serves 6 to 8

Hash

- **2 pounds russet or Yukon Gold potatoes**
- **2 pounds leftover meats (lamb, pork, and/or chicken are best)**
- **¼ pound lightly salted bacon**
- **1 onion, peeled and cut in wedges**
- **2 garlic cloves, peeled**
- **Handful parsley leaves**
- **¼ cup olive oil**
- **1 cup chicken broth or milk, heated**
- **2 teaspoons salt**
- **Freshly ground pepper**
- **⅓ cup grated Gruyère**
- **1 teaspoon butter or margarine**

In a saucepan, cover the potatoes with cold salted water and bring to a boil. Partially cover and cook for 30 minutes, or until tender.

Grind the meats, bacon, onion, garlic cloves, and parsley in a meat grinder with the coarse blade. You should have about 4 to 5 cups of ground mixture.

Heat the oil in a large skillet, add the ground meat mixture and seasonings, and stir occasionally for 10 minutes.

Preheat the oven to 350 degrees.

(continued)

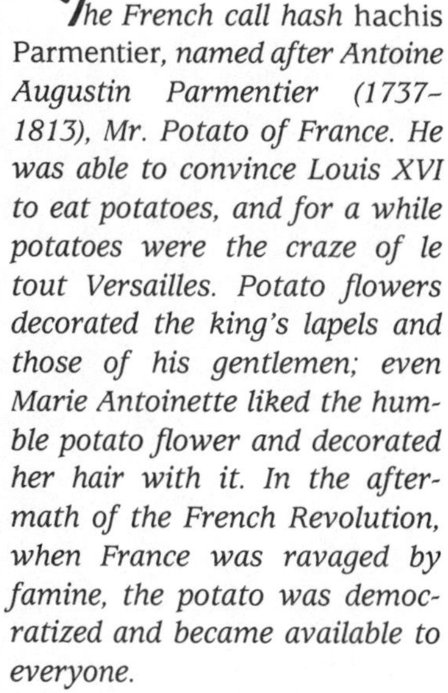

The French call hash hachis Parmentier, *named after Antoine Augustin Parmentier (1737–1813), Mr. Potato of France. He was able to convince Louis XVI to eat potatoes, and for a while potatoes were the craze of le tout Versailles. Potato flowers decorated the king's lapels and those of his gentlemen; even Marie Antoinette liked the humble potato flower and decorated her hair with it. In the aftermath of the French Revolution, when France was ravaged by famine, the potato was democratized and became available to everyone.*

Drain and peel the potatoes while still hot; mash them with a potato masher, ricer, or through a sieve. Gradually mix in the hot broth or milk. You should have about 4 to 5 cups of mashed potatoes. Mix the meats and the mashed potatoes together and season with salt and freshly ground pepper, tasting as you go along.

Pour the mixture in a greased 3-quart baking dish. Sprinkle with grated Gruyère and dots of butter or margarine. Bake in the oven for 15 minutes, or until the hash is golden brown.

Serve immediately with a tossed green salad.

NOTE: My mother mixed the ground meats and the mashed potatoes together, but the hash can also be constructed of layers of mashed potatoes and ground meats, with mashed potatoes as a top crust.

Serves 4

6. Mashed Potatoes

For good mashed potatoes, start with a starchy potato like the Russet Burbank (the Idaho baking potato), which is available all year around and is found in all supermarkets. Large Yukon Gold potatoes will also make good mashed potatoes.

I generally peel and cube the potatoes before cooking them. I cover them with a large amount of water and bring them to a boil. I cook them partially covered for 20 minutes, checking them frequently by piercing with the blade of a knife. As soon as they pierce easily but are still firm, I drain and mash them. Cooked potatoes should never stay in water or they will become waterlogged and will mash into glue. I prefer this cooking method to baking the whole potato in the oven because it is faster. The potatoes can be baked in a microwave for the fraction of that time, but according to Barbara Kafka, the most knowledgeable and intelligent food writer on microwave cooking, potatoes "do something funny in the microwave;" they don't behave the way they should. "They will have a somewhat firm, waxy texture," difficult to mash.

Milk and butter are the essential ingredients for superb mashed potatoes. But these days, when so many of us are diet- or health-conscious, we are reluctant to make old-fashioned mashed potatoes. We substitute skim milk and add a miscroscopic amount of margarine. The result is not superb.

However, don't give up on mashed potatoes; there are ways of making them taste good without milk or butter. For this method, I do not peel the potatoes before cooking them because the mashed potatoes are moistened with the water in which they

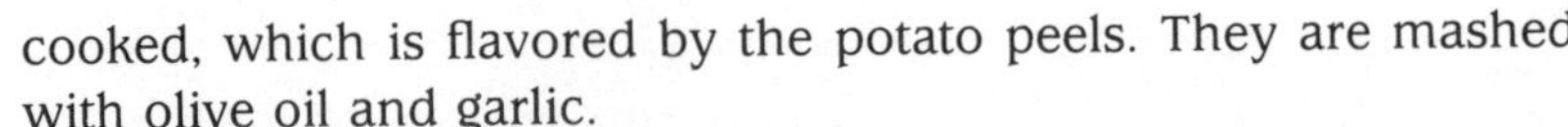

cooked, which is flavored by the potato peels. They are mashed with olive oil and garlic.

Many cooks prefer making mashed potatoes with Yukon Gold potatoes because of their yellow flesh, making believe that the yellow color replaces butter! I agree that the potato has very good flavor, but to say that it tastes buttery . . . well, it doesn't.

Each cook has her or his own way of mashing potatoes. Some swear by the ricer, others love an old-fashioned potato masher, I prefer mashing them through my kitchen strainer. But we all agree not to mash them in the food processor.

Just remember that mashed potatoes are best eaten as soon as they are made. Better to wait for them than the other way around.

Garlic Mashed Potatoes with Olive Oil

2 pounds russet or Yukon Gold potatoes
8 large unpeeled garlic cloves
1 1/2 teaspoons salt
Freshly ground pepper
1/4 cup extra-virgin olive oil

Cover the potatoes and garlic cloves with cold salted water. Bring to a boil, partially cover, and cook for 30 minutes, or until tender.

Drain the potatoes and garlic. Boil the potato water and reduce to 1 cup.

Peel the potatoes and the garlic. Mash them in the cooking pot with a potato masher, a ricer, or through a strainer back into the pot. Turn on the heat and whisk in enough potato water to bring the potatoes to a thick, creamy consistency. Season with salt and freshly ground pepper.

Heat the olive oil. At the table, pour 1 tablespoon of hot oil on each portion.

Serves 4

This recipe is the answer for all mashed potato lovers who are on strict low-cholesterol diets. Olive oil is a great no-cholesterol substitute for butter. Garlic is good for the heart and is thought to lower high blood pressure. Henry IV of France used to eat a garlic clove before courting. You can't miss with these mashed potatoes.

The first time I ate mashed potatoes with olive oil was several years ago at La Raviole in Paris, where Chef Alain Raye had just moved his restaurant from Albertville (1992 Winter Olympic site) in Savoie. I fell in love instantly with his version of mashed potatoes, garlic, and olive oil.

Mashed Potatoes Anna

...l de Pomiane, a French doctor and gastronome, said he met Anna (I suspect she is fictitious) in Paris in the thirties where she was a bonne à tout faire, *meaning she cleaned, cooked, and took care of her mistress. Anna was a simple soul who was born aboard a boat named* Anna *on the high seas between Ireland and the coast of France. She was abandoned in France, and given the name of the boat. For many years, she was a farm girl who was taken advantage of by the locals; a son was born to her. She left her son in the hands of the local priest and went to Paris to make a better living for herself and her son. She had the soul of a cook. Though barely literate, she did manage to write down all her recipes with wonderful comments on each. Edouard de Pomiane edited (or wrote) her* carnet, *as she called her treasure. Her recipes are few, but each is indeed a treasure.*

Here are her comments on "La Purée de Pommes de Terre": "Mashed potatoes, that's my forte. I make it practically every day. I make it very fast. With loin lamb chops, there is nothing better."

2 pounds russet or Yukon Gold potatoes, peeled and cut into 2-inch cubes (5 cups)
1 cup milk
4 tablespoons (½ stick) unsalted butter
⅓ cup heavy cream
1½ teaspoons salt
Freshly ground pepper

. In a large saucepan, cover the potatoes with cold salted water. Bring to a boil, partially cover, and cook for 20 minutes, or until the potatoes are tender.

Scald the milk. Drain the potatoes and mash them in the cooking pot with a potato masher, a ricer, or through a strainer back into the pot. Turn on the heat and gradually whisk in the hot milk, butter, and cream. Season with salt and freshly ground pepper and serve immediately.

Serves 4

Mashed Potatoes Helene

2 pounds russet or Yukon Gold potatoes, peeled and cut into 2-inch cubes (5 cups)
½ cup milk
4 tablespoons (½ stick) unsalted butter
1 cup freshly grated Emmenthal cheese
1½ teaspoons salt
Freshly ground pepper

This Helene is a Parisian lady who loves to make mashed potatoes with Emmenthal, a good imported Swiss cheese.

In a large saucepan, cover the potatoes with cold salted water. Bring to a boil, partially cover, and cook for 20 minutes, or until tender.

Scald the milk. Drain the potatoes and mash them in the cooking pot with a potato masher, a ricer, or through a strainer back into the pot. Turn on the heat and whisk the hot milk and butter into the mashed potatoes.

Off the heat, fold in the freshly grated Emmenthal cheese. Season with salt and freshly ground pepper. Serve immediately.

Serves 4

Colcannon

IRISH MASHED POTATOES

1 pound kale, stems removed and leaves chopped (2 cups cooked)
2½ teaspoons salt
4 pounds russet or Yukon Gold potatoes, peeled and cut into 1-inch cubes (10 cups)
1½ cups milk
8 tablespoons (1 stick) unsalted butter, at room temperature
Freshly ground pepper

Wash the kale under cold water, drain, and place in a pan with ¼ cup water and ½ teaspoon salt. Cover tightly. Braise for 15 minutes, checking once in a while that the kale does not burn. Chop fine or process in the food processor until fine.

In a large saucepan, cover the potatoes with cold salted water. Bring to a boil, partially cover, and cook for 30 minutes, or until tender.

Drain the potatoes and mash them in the cooking pot with a potato masher, a ricer, or through a strainer back into the pot.

Turn on the heat and fold the kale into the mashed potatoes. Gradually whisk in the milk and butter. Season with the remaining 2 teaspoons salt and freshly ground pepper. Serve immediately.

Serves 8

In Scotland and in Ireland colcannon is served at Halloween. The Irish name colcannon comes from the Gaelic "cal ceann fhionnn," which means white cabbage. It can be made with cabbage but it is traditionally made with kale, perhaps the first cabbage to be cultivated. In Scotland, it is called colcannon and kilkenny, and in Wales it is the tongue twister rumbledethumps.

At Halloween, the Irish in the south of Ireland place one of the following in the colcannon: a gold or brass ring, a sixpence, a thimble, or a button, wrapped in a piece of wax paper. The person who finds the ring is supposed to be married within the year. The sixpence is to make the person rich in a year; the thimble represents spinsterhood, and the button, bachelorhood.

My Irish friend Bernadette reports, "I served colcannon to my family one year when I had only dimes to offer. I wrapped up the dimes and put them in everyone's colcannon; after dinner, I came up thirty cents short, but everyone had cleaned off their plates. I packed the four children and my husband into the station wagon and off we went to the doctor, who enjoyed our visit immensely."

Mashed Potatoes with Scallions

1 cup chopped scallions, or ½ cup minced chives
½ cup milk

In a pan, cover the scallions with milk and bring to a boil. (If using chives, they go in later.) Partially cover and cook over medium heat until the scallions are soft, about 10 minutes.

Follow the directions for colcannon but instead of adding kale, combine the potatoes with the cooked scallions or the minced chives.

Several Irish and Scottish cookbooks give various names to a variation of colcannon: champ, stelk, cally, poundies, or pandy. Instead of kale, scallions or chives are combined with the mashed potatoes. It's great.

Mashed Potatoes with Salsify

Every season brings a new crop of vegetables to the market. The fall brings such root vegetables as salsify, parsnip, turnip, yellow rutabaga, and celery root. All these vegetables cooked with potatoes make wonderful and unusual mashed potatoes.

Salsify is a long, slender vegetable shaped like a parsnip. A friend of mine describes it as a celery root that went on a diet. This Quasimodo of the vegetable world has a delicate texture. It is not as sweet as a parsnip and has a faint flavor of oyster; in fact it is sometimes called oyster plant. The Chinese use it to make oyster sauce.

To prepare salsify, I put on kitchen gloves (surgical liners) to avoid staining my hands, brush off the dirt, then scrub the salsify under running cold water. I peel them with a vegetable peeler and immediately put the salsify in water acidulated with lemon juice to keep them from turning dark.

1 pound salsify, peeled and cut in 1-inch slices (3 cups)
Milk
2 pounds russet or Yukon Gold potatoes, peeled and cut into 2-inch cubes (5 cups)
1/3 cup heavy cream, or 3 tablespoons olive oil
2 teaspoons salt
Freshly ground pepper

In a large saucepan, cover the salsify with milk and cook over medium heat while peeling and cutting the potatoes. Add the potatoes to the salsify after 30 minutes (salsify take longer to cook than potatoes). Cook over medium heat until the vegetables are tender. Drain.

Mash the potatoes and salsify in the cooking pot with a potato masher, a ricer, or through a strainer back into the pot. Turn on the heat and whisk in cream or olive oil. Season with salt and freshly ground pepper. Serve immediately.

Serves 6

Mashed Potatoes with Celery Root

2½ pounds celery root, peeled and cut into 1-inch cubes (6 cups)
2½ pounds russet or Yukon Gold potatoes, peeled and cut into 1-inch cubes (6 cups)
1 garlic clove, peeled
1 cup milk
4 to 5 tablespoons unsalted butter
1½ teaspoons salt
Freshly ground pepper
Cranberry Sauce (recipe follows)

In a large pan, cover the vegetables and garlic with cold salted water and bring to a boil. Partially cover and cook for 20 minutes, or until tender.

Drain. Mash the vegetables in the cooking pot with a potato masher, a ricer, or through a strainer back into the pot. Reheat and gradually whisk in the milk and butter. Season with salt and freshly ground pepper.

Make a nest in the mashed vegetables and pour in the cranberry sauce. Serve immediately.

Makes 8 servings

CRANBERRY SAUCE

½ cup sugar
½ cup water
1 cup fresh cranberries

Combine the sugar and water in a saucepan and bring to a boil. Boil 5 minutes to thicken the syrup. Add the cranberries and simmer uncovered over low to medium heat, without stirring, for 5 minutes.

The best season for celery root is late fall and early winter. It is superb mashed with potatoes and served with a cranberry sauce. The dish becomes festive as well as delicious. It is a must for Thanksgiving.

Sour Creamed Mashed Potatoes with French Onion Rings

This is a specialty of Shirley Blackmar from Sewickley, Pennsylvania, who found this very interesting recipe in The Three Rivers Cook Book, *a collection put together by the ladies of Sewickley. The sweet and sour tastes of onions and sour cream make these mashed potatoes unusual and good.*

2 pounds russet or Yukon Gold potatoes, peeled and cut into 2-inch cubes (5 cups)
2 tablespoons butter or margarine
1 cup sour cream
1 teaspoon salt
Freshly ground pepper
French Onion Rings (recipe follows)

Preheat the oven to 350 degrees; butter a 2-quart baking dish.

In a large saucepan, cover the potatoes with cold salted water. Bring to a boil, partially cover, and cook for 20 minutes, or until tender.

Drain the potatoes and mash them in the cooking pot with a potato masher, a ricer, or through a strainer back into the pot.

Turn on the heat and whisk in the butter and sour cream. Season with salt and freshly ground pepper.

Transfer the mashed potatoes to the prepared baking dish and top with onion rings. Bake for 15 minutes and serve immediately.

Serves 4

FRENCH ONION RINGS

1 cup flour
3 large eggs
½ cup beer
½ teaspoon salt
1 tablespoon brandy
1 medium yellow onion
1 quart corn oil

I make the batter 1 hour before cooking the potatoes and deep-fry the onion rings while the potatoes are cooking.

Put the flour in a large bowl, make a well, and break the eggs into the well. Mix in the eggs, beer, and ½ cup water until the batter is free of lumps. Stir in the salt. Set aside for 1 hour. Just before frying, stir in the brandy.

Cut the onion into ¼-inch-thick slices; separate the rings.

Heat the corn oil to 325 degrees. Dip the onion rings in the batter and deep-fry until golden brown (about 2 or 3 minutes). Drain and put on top of the mashed potatoes.

Mashed Potatoes with Yellow Turnips, Bacon, and Parsley

I remember eating yellow turnips (rutabagas in French) during World War II, and hoping I would never have to eat them again in my life. Here I am, eating and loving them. If you have never eaten or cooked them, I must warn you that while cooking, turnips emit a strong odor. Don't give up; the taste is much different from the odor.

1 pound russet or Yukon Gold potatoes, peeled and cut into 1-inch cubes (2½ cups)
1 pound yellow turnips, peeled and cut into 1-inch cubes (2½ cups)
6 slices bacon
4 tablespoons (½ stick) butter or margarine
¼ cup minced fresh parsley
½ teaspoon salt
Freshly ground pepper

In a large saucepan, cover the potatoes and turnips with cold salted water. Bring to a boil, partially cover, and cook for 20 minutes, or until very tender.

Cook 6 slices of bacon until crisp. Drain on paper towels. Crumble the bacon and set aside.

Drain the vegetables and mash them in the cooking pot with a potato masher, a ricer, or through a strainer back into the pot. Turn the heat on and whisk in the butter or margarine and parsley. Fold in the bacon and season with salt and freshly ground pepper. Serve immediately.

Serves 4

Sweet Potato Purée

1½ pounds russet potatoes
2 pounds sweet potatoes
4 tablespoons (½ stick) unsalted butter, cut up
1 teaspoon or more salt
Freshly ground pepper

Preheat the oven to 400 degrees.

Bake the white potatoes for 1 hour and the sweet potatoes for 45 minutes. Split the potatoes and scoop out the pulp with a spoon. Mash them through a strainer into a saucepan, pressing with the back of a large spoon.

Reheat the mashed potatoes, stirring with a wooden spoon. Remove from the heat and gradually add the butter. Season with salt and freshly ground pepper.

Serves 4 to 6

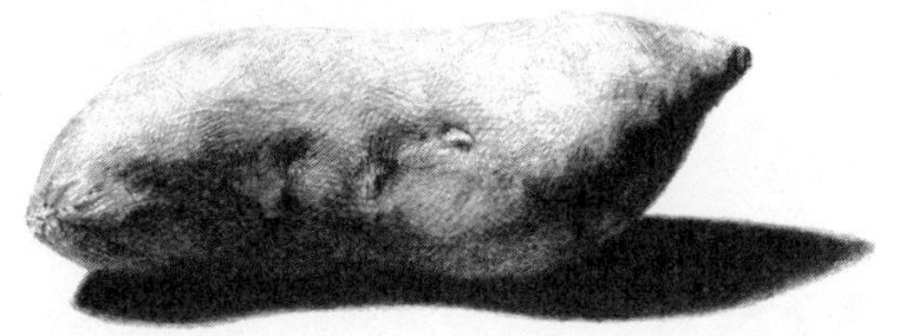

These splendid mashed sweet potatoes mixed with baking potatoes are the perfect accompaniment to my Thanksgiving turkey. I thank Richard Olney for this recipe and for all the techniques I learned from his works. In 1967, when I studied at L'Ecole des trois gourmandes in Paris, the cooking school founded by Simone Beck, Louisette Bertholle, and Julia Child, I was told by Mme Bertholle to read an "amusing" column in Cuisine et Vins de France, *the magazine founded by Curnonsky and Madeleine Decure. Richard Olney in "Un Americain Gourmand à Paris" explained in great detail how to prepare a seasonal dinner every month; sometimes the menus were elaborate and sometimes very simple, but the results were always perfect. Most of the menus have since been published in the* French Menu Cookbook. *I finally met Richard in 1975 at my friend Cecily Brownstone's house. I made a gratin of leeks and grilled skirt steaks in the fireplace; we drank, talked, and began a long friendship.*

7.

Baked, Sautéed, Braised, and Roasted Potatoes

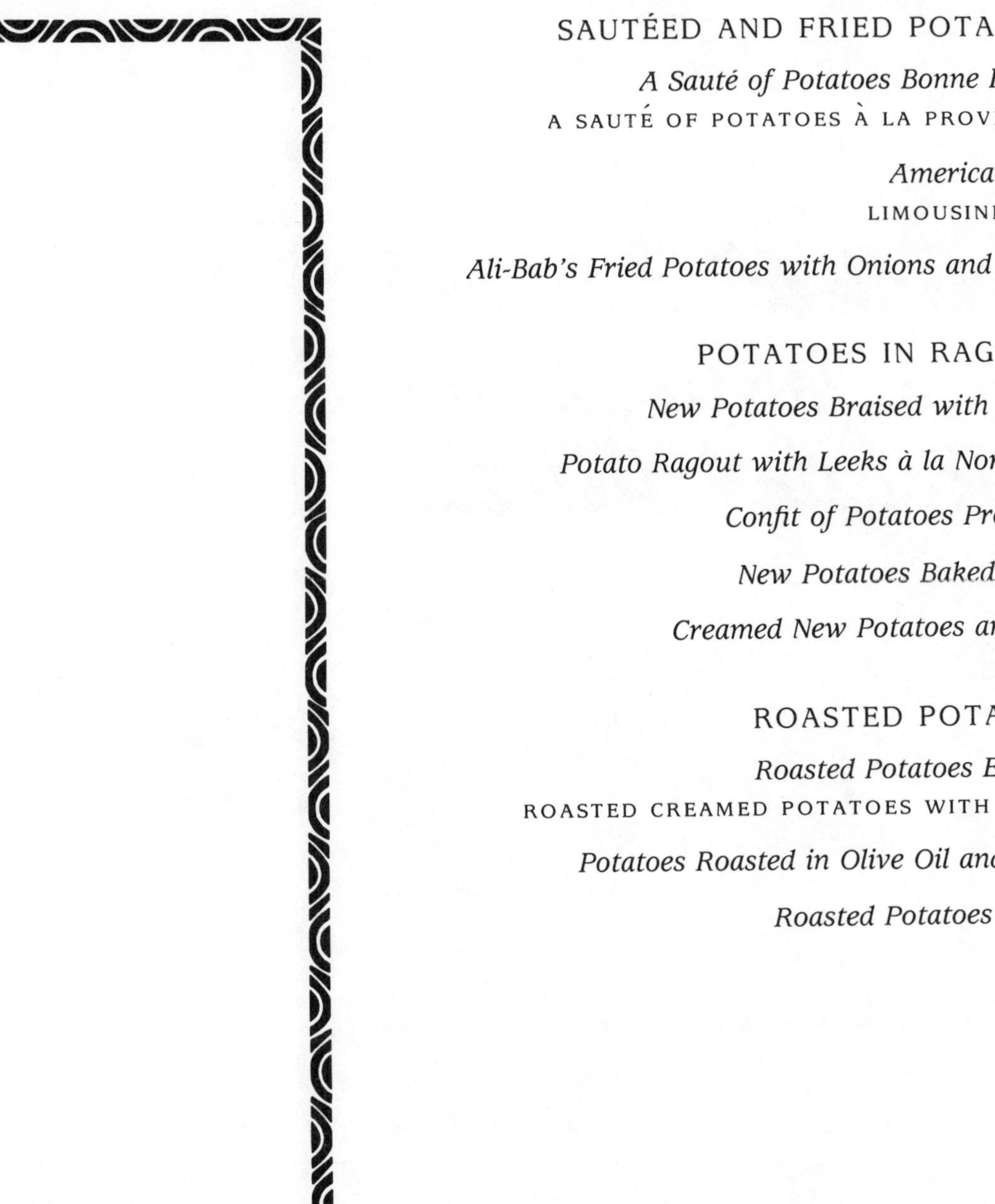

BAKING POTATOES

The baked potato is as American as apple pie. The Irish have their stews, the Germans their dumplings, the French their gratins, the Italians their gnocchi, and the Americans their baked potato. Nowhere else do baking potatoes taste better than in an American kitchen.

The russet potato (see page xviii for its history), grown in Idaho and other states, makes the best baked potato.

Choose potatoes of roughly the same size, each weighing about 1/2 pound. Bake at 425 degrees for 1 hour; prick the skin of each potato at half time, letting the steam escape. The starch in the potato will expand in the hot oven, creating a fluffy inside and a perfectly dry crisp skin. Wrapping potatoes in aluminum foil prevents them from becoming flaky, as too much moisture is retained.

It is acknowledged that baking potatoes in a microwave is not ideal, as the potatoes don't seem to taste as good; but there are times when it has to be done. This is the microwave technique used by most of my microwave friends: Bake on high for 7 minutes. Then wrap the potato in aluminum foil, shiny side inside, and leave at room temperature for 10 more minutes to finish baking.

The next best thing to the hot potato itself is the topping, and what a choice we have! The most traditional is butter. For a delicious nonanimal-fat alternative, try 1 tablespoon very fruity olive oil. Sour cream with chives, mayonnaise, brandade, or a simple dressing of chopped fresh tomatoes, basil, minced garlic, and fruity olive oil are all great treats.

Classic Baked Potatoes

- 6 russet potatoes, weighing ½ pound each
- 1 teaspoon oil
- 6 tablespoons (¾ stick) butter or margarine
- Salt

Preheat oven to 425 degrees.

Scrub the potatoes under cold running water. Pat dry and brush lightly with oil. Place on a rack fitted in the broiler pan.

Bake for 30 minutes on the middle shelf of the oven.

Puncture the skin of the potatoes all over, letting the steam escape. Bake for 30 minutes more.

Eat as soon as they are taken out of the oven. Cut 2 short gashes, one crosswise and one lengthwise and squeeze the potato with both hands before adding butter or margarine and salt. Serve immediately.

Serves 6

Baked Potatoes Franco-American

I found this recipe in a 1940 cookbook, The Philadelphia Cook Book of Town and Country *by Anna Wethevill Reed. It's the virtual duplicate of an eighteenth-century French potato recipe of Parmentier (see page 99). Parmentier used fines herbes instead of chives, but the technique is identical.*

To provide plenty of stuffing, I bake an extra potato.

- 5 russet potatoes, weighing about ½ pound each
- 1 teaspoon oil
- 5 tablespoons butter
- ⅓ cup minced chives
- 1 teaspoon or more salt
- Freshly ground pepper

Preheat the oven to 425 degrees.

Scrub the potatoes clean and rub the oil on their skins.

Bake in the middle of the oven for 30 minutes. Puncture the skins to let the steam escape, and bake for 30 minutes more.

Split the potatoes in two lenghthwise. Scoop out the flesh and mash it with an old-fashioned potato masher, a ricer, or through a strainer, with 4 tablespoons of the butter.

Fold the minced chives into the potatoes and season with salt and freshly ground pepper. Fill the shells of 4 potatoes with the mashed potatoes.

Dot with the remaining butter and bake for 5 more minutes. Serve immediately.

Serves 4

Potatoes Baked on a Bed of Rock Salt

6 russet potatoes, weighing ½ pound each
1 teaspoon salt
1 tablespoon fresh thyme leaves, or 1 teaspoon dried thyme
3 large garlic cloves, peeled and cut into 8 slivers each
Kosher salt

Preheat the oven to 425 degrees.

Split each potato in half lengthwise. With the point of a knife, make incisions all over the potato flesh.

Combine the salt and thyme. Dip each garlic sliver in the mixture. Insert the thyme-garlic slivers in the incisions. Reshape each potato and secure it with wooden toothpicks. Place in a pan lined with a ½-inch-thick layer of kosher salt.

Bake in the hot oven for 1 hour. Brush off the salt and serve immediately. You can reuse the salt.

Serves 6

Pommes Maxime

Several great French restaurants are known for their potato dishes. Many take on the name of the restaurant. Pommes Maxime are the signature of Maxim's in Paris. Pommes Gaufrettes Troisgros are made in the restaurant Troisgros in Roanne, an hour from Lyon. La Mère Blanc's pancakes are made at La Mère Blanc in Vonnas; and Jamin in Paris is well known for its delicious mashed potatoes with butter.

1 pound White Rose or Yukon Gold potatoes, peeled and sliced 1/16 inch thick (3 cups)
6 tablespoons (3/4 stick) margarine or clarified butter
2 teaspoons salt
Freshly ground pepper

Preheat the oven to 425 degrees.

Wash the potato slices in a large bowl of cold water. Drain and wash once more under running cold water. Pat each slice dry separately.

In a large bowl, toss the potato slices and the clarified butter or margarine together with your hands.

Butter a large baking pan. I use my broiler pan—it's large and has low sides. Overlap the potatoes in one single layer.

Bake in the oven for 20 minutes, or until golden brown. Sprinkle with salt and freshly ground pepper and serve immediately.

At Maxim's the potatoes are served on linen napkins, which soak up the butter.

Serves 4

Pommes Gaufrettes Troisgros

WAFFLED POTATO CHIPS

These chips are similar to Maxim's, but the potatoes are sliced with ridges to produce *gaufrettes*—waffled chips.

Trim the potatoes on all sides to shape them into rectangles as for potato puffs (see page 150).

Cut the potatoes into 1/16-inch-thick slices, using a slicer with a rippled blade.

Soak the potatoes overnight, or for several hours, changing the water occasionally.

Preheat the oven to 425 degrees.

Drain and pat dry. In a large bowl, toss the potatoes with the clarified butter or margarine. Overlap them in a large broiler pan. Bake 15 minutes.

Drain the butter and continue baking the potatoes until golden. Drain the remaining butter, sprinkle with salt and serve immediately.

Pommes Anna is the most delicious and prettiest potato cake. Layers and layers of paper-thin potato slices are packed in a mold and baked with a large amount of melted butter (you may substitute margarine), salt, and pepper. The cake is golden brown and crunchy on the outside, moist and buttery inside.

I am giving 3 versions of this cake, the traditional recipe, my aunt's variation, and the recipe of Marc Meneau, who substitutes oil for butter and bakes the cake in an oil bath. All 3 versions are excellent.

Pommes Anna is so beloved by the French that they have even given the name to the dish in which the potatoes are cooked. The pan is made of heavy-gauge copper and is in 2 pieces: the bottom part is smaller than the top, which is used as a lid and serving dish. When the potato cake is baked, it is inverted into the lid, which, with its 2 brass handles, is transformed into a serving dish.

I bake my Anna in a 9-inch cast-iron skillet with great success. I cut off the ends of the potatoes to make even slices (I

Classic Potato Anna

3 pounds Yukon Gold or russet potatoes, peeled and cut in slices between 1/16 inch and 1/8 inch thick (8 cups)
3/4 cup (1 1/2 sticks) unsalted butter or margarine, melted
2 teaspoons salt
Freshly ground pepper

Preheat oven to 425 degrees.

Wash the potato slices in a large bowl of cold water. Drain and pat dry on several layers of paper or linen towels.

Overlap the first layer of potatoes, starting at the center of the pan. Sprinkle with salt and pepper, and pour melted butter over every layer of potatoes from then on. Occasionally, push down on the potato layers with a pancake turner.

When the pan is full, cover it with buttered aluminum foil, cut to fit exactly on top of the potatoes.

Bake in the middle shelf of the oven for 30 minutes. Remove the aluminum foil and bake for another 30 minutes, or until the potatoes are golden brown.

Loosen the bottom layer of potatoes with a flexible blade if necessary. This next step is a little tricky: Invert the potato cake

onto a flat serving dish, keeping it slightly askew so the butter can drain into a bowl. Reserve the drained butter for another use, or freeze it and use it again for your next potato Anna (you'll want to make it again and again).

Cut the cake in wedges with a pair of scissors (easier than using a knife). Serve immediately.

Serves 6

either make soup with the potato ends or I parboil them first and stir-fry them). I make about 8 layers of potatoes in a 9-inch skillet, generously buttered.

Tatane's Potato Anna with Herbs and Cheese

Potato Anna
½ cup minced fresh chives and parsley
1½ cups grated Gruyère
½ cup melted margarine

Follow the potato Anna recipe but add cheese and herbs between layers and pour margarine instead of butter on the layers.

This recipe is my aunt's version of Potato Anna. Tatane was my teacher in the kitchen. She always used margarine instead of butter, because butter was so precious to her that she only ate it unadorned, like a piece of cake.

Meneau's Potato Anna

Marc Meneau is unusual among today's great French chefs. He was a businessman who decided in his late twenties to switch careers. Very quickly, his restaurant in St. Père en Vézelay, in Burgundy, became a great spot to eat.

In his version of potato Anna, the cake is baked in an oil bath, which gives it a specially crunchy top and bottom. For this version I use a round cake pan 8 inches in diameter with sides 2 inches high, which I fit into a 10-inch pan. I pour enough oil in between the pans to reach halfway up the sides of the smaller pan. And to be absolutely sure that no oil will spill in the oven, I put the 2 pans on a jelly roll pan.

4 ounces bacon strips
2 pounds Yukon Gold or russet potatoes, peeled and sliced between 1/8 inch and 1/16 inch thick (6 cups)
1/2 cup grated Parmesan
2 teaspoons salt
Freshly ground pepper
1/3 cup olive oil

FOR THE OIL BATH:
About 2 cups vegetable oil

Preheat the oven to 400 degrees; line an 8- by 2-inch cake pan with wax paper and lightly oil the paper.

Cook the bacon until crisp. Drain on paper towels. Crumble the bacon and set aside.

Plunge the potato slices into boiling water. Drain and plunge in a bowl of cold water. Pat dry with towels.

Layer the potatoes, overlapping them, starting from the center of the pan. Sprinkle every second layer with Parmesan, bacon, salt, and pepper. As you layer them, press down to even out the potatoes in the pan. (I use a meat pounder to do this.) Pour 1/3 cup olive oil over the potato cake.

Put the potatoes over low heat for 5 minutes. Place the cake pan in a 10-inch pan and pour enough oil between the pans to come about halfway up the sides of the potato cake pan.

Bake for 45 minutes, or until the potatoes are golden brown. Very carefully, with potholders or tongs, lift the potato cake pan out of the oil bath. Cool slightly before unmolding.

Cut the cake in wedges with a pair of scissors (easier than using a knife). Serve immediately.

Serves 4 to 6

Potatoes Byron

6 russet potatoes, weighing ½ pound each
6 tablespoons (¾ stick) unsalted butter or margarine
Vegetable oil
1½ teaspoons salt
Freshly ground pepper
1 teaspoon ground cumin
½ cup half and half
½ cup freshly grated cheese (Gruyère, Parmesan, or Cheddar)

A creation of Alexandre Dumaine, who was one of the great French chefs of this century. The baked potatoes are mashed, seasoned with butter and cumin, shaped into a cake, and browned in the oven with cheese and cream. It's elegant for a dinner party.

Preheat the oven to 425 degrees; butter a 4-cup soufflé mold or bowl.

Oil each potato and bake in the center of the preheated oven for 30 minutes. Prick the potato skin all over and bake for 30 more minutes.

Split the potatoes in two. Scoop out the pulp with a spoon. (You can snack on the skins.) Mash the butter into the pulp with a fork. Mix in the salt, pepper, and cumin. Taste and correct seasoning.

To shape the potatoes for a classic presentation, pack the mixture into a 4-cup buttered soufflé mold or bowl. Unmold the potatoes onto an ovenproof serving dish. Cover with half and half and sprinkle with the cheese. Bake in the center of the oven until the top browns, about 5 minutes. For a simpler version, mound the potatoes without molding before browning.

Serves 6

SAUTÉED AND FRIED POTATOES

An all-purpose or boiling potato is best for sautéing or stir-frying, as it does not disintegrate during cooking as a baking potato would. I prefer a yellow flesh potato like the Yukon Gold, Yellow Finnish, or Bintje; of the white flesh potatoes, I like the Red Pontiac, or Nordland, or the White Rose potato from the West Coast.

The best time for these potatoes is summer and early fall.

A Sauté of Potatoes Bonne Femme

Potatoes quickly sautéed in oil and sprinkled with a mixture of garlic and parsley are in the domaine of what the French call cuisine bonne femme. A bonne femme is a homemaker who has the knack of preparing simple and delicious dishes on the spur of the moment, as well as cooking long-simmering dishes when she has the time. Jeanine, the

2 pounds Red Nordland, Red Pontiac, Yukon Gold, or White Rose potatoes, peeled and diced into ¼-inch cubes (6 cups)
⅓ cup corn oil
2 tablespoons minced parsley mixed with 1 tablespoon minced garlic
Salt
Freshly ground pepper

In a pan, cover the potatoes with cold salted water and bring to a boil; turn off the heat and drain the potatoes.

In a 10-inch nonstick skillet, heat 3 tablespoons oil and sauté (stir-fry) half the potatoes for 15 minutes, or until they are fork-tender, shaking the skillet most of the time.

Transfer the potatoes to a serving platter. Heat the remaining oil and stir-fry the remaining potatoes; or sauté all the potatoes in 2 skillets.

Put all the potatoes back into 1 skillet and sprinkle with the mixture of minced parsley and garlic. Stir-fry for 1 minute. Season with salt and freshly ground pepper. Serve immediately.

Serves 4

giver of this recipe, brings the potatoes to a boil before she sautés them in oil. As most French cooks do, she uses huile d'arachide, *a type of peanut oil less strong than American peanut oil. I use corn oil.*

To properly sauté potatoes, there should never be more than 3 cups of potatoes at a time in a 9- to 10-inch skillet; to speed up the cooking, I have 2 skillets going at once. Cooking times depend on the variety of potato, though 10 to 15 minutes for fork-tender potatoes is average.

A Sauté of Potatoes à la Provençale

4 tablespoons (½ stick) butter, softened
Several strands saffron, softened in 1 teaspoon water
⅓ cup olive oil
2 pounds potatoes, peeled, diced, and parboiled as in previous recipe
4 large garlic cloves, peeled and cut into ¼-inch slivers
Salt
Freshly ground pepper
¼ cup minced parsley

Mix butter and saffron together and refrigerate to firm up the butter for at least 1 hour.

Heat the oil in 2 large skillets and toss in the potatoes. Stir-fry for 10 minutes, or until the potatoes are almost fork-tender. Toss in the garlic and stir-fry for 5 minutes more. Season with salt and pepper.

Sprinkle parsley over the potatoes and serve with the saffron butter, sliced into patties.

Serves 4

American fries are pan-fried slices of potatoes. Marilyn Dabner, my sister-in-law who lives in Oklahoma, is my expert on such traditional American potato recipes as hash browns, creamed potatoes with peas, and this recipe, which she calls American fries. She used to slice the potatoes but did not wash the slices to rinse off the surface starch; she had never heard of doing it. I told her if they were washed, the fries would be crisper. So we tested the 2 methods at the same time in nonstick skillets. Indeed, the washed slices of potatoes were crisper. It is a matter of taste. I like them both but she prefers the crisper ones!

Do not fry more than 1 pound of potato slices (3 cups) at a time in a 10-inch skillet, otherwise the slices will not fry evenly and some of them will steam.

American Fries

1/4 pound bacon
2 pounds Yukon Gold, Red Pontiac, Red Nordland, or White Rose potatoes, peeled and sliced 1/8 inch thick (6 cups)
2 onions, peeled and coarsely chopped
2 teaspoons salt
Freshly ground pepper

In 2 nonstick 10-inch skillets, divide the bacon slices and fry until crisp. Remove the bacon with a slotted spoon and set aside, leaving the fat in the pan.

If you wash the potato slices, pat dry in a kitchen towel.

In the hot bacon fat, stir-fry 3 cups of potato slices in each skillet for 3 minutes or so. Stir in the onions and season with salt and freshly ground pepper. Partially cover each pan and cook over low to medium heat for 15 to 20 minutes, stirring the potatoes occasionally.

Crumble the bacon, add it to the potatoes, and serve immediately.

Serves 4

Limousine Fries

American Fries (preceding recipe)
¼ cup minced parsley
½ pound mushrooms (cèpes or shiitake), coarsely chopped

Follow the directions for American fries, substituing goose or chicken fat for bacon fat. Add the minced parsley with the onions and cook the potatoes, partially covered, for 20 minutes, stirring occasionally.

Uncover, raise the heat, and stir-fry the mushrooms with the potatoes for 5 minutes. Serve immediately.

In the Limousine region of central France, I found a recipe that reminds me very much of American fries. The potatoes are fried in goose fat instead of bacon fat. In the fall, the potatoes are mixed with fresh cèpes (porcini). Substitute shiitake or any exotic mushrooms if cèpes are not available.

Ali-Bab's Fried Potatoes with Onions and Chives

Ali-Bab (a nom de plume) was a Polish count who emigrated to France in the nineteenth century. An engineer by trade, he was a "gourmand" and a "gourmet" by inspiration. He traveled all over the world for his work and wrote a treatise on how to eat well, Gastronomie Pratique.

1 pound unpeeled Yukon Gold, Red Nordland, Red Pontiac, or White Rose potatoes, sliced 1/8 inch thick (3 cups)
1 teaspoon kosher salt
1/2 cup corn oil
Salt
Freshly ground pepper
2 tablespoons unsalted butter or margarine
1 medium onion, peeled and thinly sliced
1 tablespoon minced fresh chives

Wash the potato slices in cold water. Pat dry. Sprinkle the kosher salt over the slices, which will draw out more water. Let stand for 10 minutes. Once more pat dry.

In a large nonstick skillet, heat the oil. Stir-fry the potato slices in the hot fat for 10-15 minutes, turning them a number of times with a pancake turner until golden brown. Season with salt and freshly ground pepper. With a slotted spoon, transfer the potatoes to a serving platter.

Discard the fat in the skillet, melt butter or margarine and stir-fry the onion slices for 5 minutes.

Toss the potatoes, onions, and chives together and serve immediately.

Serves 2

POTATOES IN RAGOUTS

Potatoes freshly dug in the spring are called baby potatoes or new potatoes. They can be steamed, boiled, and braised. Peeling is a matter of taste.

The potato varieties mostly seen in markets are the Red La Soda or La Rouge, the creamer (any variety of potatoes, no more than 1 inch in diameter), the fingerling potato, and the Ruby Crescent; the Peruvian Blue, the baby Yukon Gold, and Yellow Finnish are found in farmers' markets, specialty food stores, or in your neighbor's garden if you happen to be so lucky. The Ruby Crescent is the potato that resembles in shape and taste the French potato *La Ratte*, currently the most prized potato in France.

New Potatoes Braised with Thyme

¼ cup virgin olive oil
1½ pounds Red La Soda or La Rouge potatoes, quartered
1 sprig fresh thyme
1 teaspoon salt
Freshly ground pepper

Heat the olive oil in a large nonstick skillet and stir-fry the potatoes for 8 minutes, shaking the pan once in a while to prevent scorching. Add the thyme and season with salt and freshly ground pepper. Cover and cook for 20 minutes over low heat, checking once in a while and letting the water gathered on the underside of the lid fall back into the potatoes.

Uncover, raise the heat, and brown the potatoes, shaking the pan. Serve right away.

Serves 2

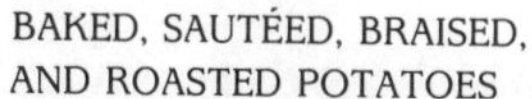

Potato Ragout with Leeks à la Normande

Normandy is the land of butter, cream, and cheeses. In this simple ragout, you can substitute margarine for butter and plain yogurt for cream, but then don't call it à la normande. *I moisten the potatoes with chicken stock; if it's not available, add the same amount of water and brown several chicken bones with the leeks and potatoes.*

4 tablespoons (½ stick) unsalted butter or margarine
Whites of 2 leeks, thinly sliced (1½ cups)
1½ pounds Red Nordland, Red Pontiac, Yukon Gold, or White Rose potatoes, peeled and cut into ¾-inch cubes (2½ cups)
¼ pound chicken backs (optional)
1 teaspoon salt
Freshly ground pepper
1 sprig fresh tarragon, or 1 teaspoon dried tarragon
1½ cups chicken stock or water
¼ cup heavy cream or plain yogurt
¼ cup minced parsley

In a dutch oven, melt the butter over medium-low heat; add the leeks and stir constantly for 1 minute. Cook another 5 minutes, watching that the leeks don't scorch.

Stir in the potatoes and add the chicken backs if you are using water instead of stock. Cook for 10 minutes, stirring and shaking the pan to prevent burning. Season with salt and freshly ground pepper.

Add tarragon and water or stock. Raise the heat to medium high and cook for 20 minutes, shaking the pan once in a while to be sure the vegetables do not scorch at the bottom of the pan.

Add the cream or yogurt and stir the ragout. Cook for another 5 to 10 minutes, or until the potatoes are tender and the liquid has thickened. Discard the tarragon sprig and the chicken backs, if any. Taste and correct seasoning.

Stir in the parsley and transfer the ragout to a heated vegetable dish. Serve immediately.

Serves 4

Confit of Potatoes Provençal

¼ cup virgin olive oil
2½ pounds fingerling potatoes or creamers, peeled
1½ teaspoons salt
Freshly ground pepper
About 1½ cups rich chicken broth

In a large skillet, heat the oil. Add the potaoes and stir-fry for 3 minutes. Sprinkle with salt and freshly ground pepper.

Pour in 1 cup of broth, lower the heat, and cook the potatoes, partially covered, until the broth is totally evaporated. If the potatoes are not tender at that stage, add more broth and continue braising until tender.

Serve immediately.

Serves 6

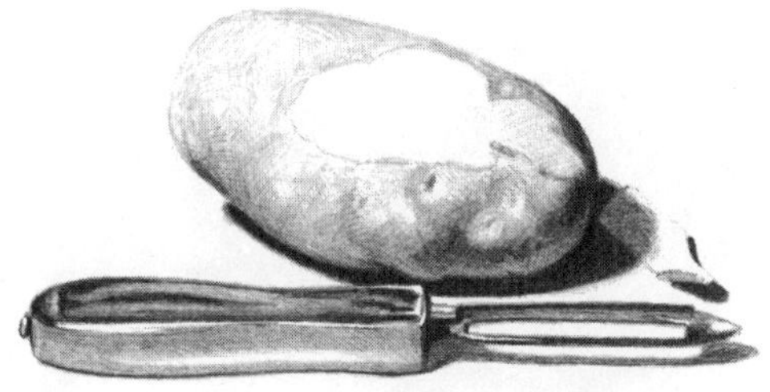

Potatoes barigoulo, *the Provençal term for vegetables cooked slowly in fat and broth, comes from a cookbook written during the French Revolution:* La Cuisinière Républicaine.

New Potatoes Baked in Salt

These potatoes are baked whole and unpeeled, buried in kosher salt; there is no fat and there is nothing better than eating them, peels and all, with a tossed green salad.

Don't be alarmed at the amount of salt used in the dish. The potatoes will not taste salty; *as a matter of fact, when the potatoes are split open, you might want to season them with more salt and freshly ground pepper! They are delicious with eggless Potato Aioli (page 27). (You can reuse the salt whenever you make these potatoes.)*

2 pounds new small Red La Rouge or La Soda, Yellow Finnish, or small Yukon Gold potatoes

5 pounds kosher salt

Preheat the oven to 450 degrees.

Pour a layer of salt 1 inch thick in the bottom of a 9-quart dutch oven. Bury some potatoes in the salt. Pour in more salt and continue to bury more potatoes, finishing with a layer of salt.

Cover the pot and bake in the middle shelf of the oven for 1 hour and 15 minutes.

Pour the contents of the dutch oven into a very large bowl, and dig out the potatoes. If the potatoes are encrusted with salt, brush it off.

Serves 6

Creamed New Potatoes and Peas

1 pound new Red La Soda, La Rouge, Yellow Finnish, small Yukon Gold, or Ruby Crescent potatoes, peeled
1 1/2 cups half and half
2 sprigs fresh tarragon
2 pounds fresh peas in pods (2 1/2 cups shelled)
1 teaspoon salt
Freshly ground pepper

Bring 1 inch of water to a boil in a large pan.

Fit a collapsible steamer into the pan and steam the potatoes until tender, 15 to 20 minutes, depending on their size.

Bring the cream slowly to a boil with the tarragon. Skim off the top of the cream, discarding the white scum.

Add the peas and simmer for 5 to 10 minutes, or until the peas are tender. Discard the tarragon and add the potatoes. Bring to a boil for 1 minute, add salt and pepper, and serve immediately.

Serves 4

My husband can't stand gardening. Why? Because as a child his parents had a vast vegetable garden that needed keeping up. Of course, he says that he had to do all the work. I doubt that because he has a brother and a sister who are both hard workers, as were his parents. Anyway, this dish was a product of their garden. His mother cooked it when the peas were ready to be picked. Freshly picked green peas and freshly dug small potatoes make this dish memorable.

When my sister-in-law gave me this recipe, I could not help adding a few sprigs of fresh tarragon with the cream. It's a lovely, easy dish to prepare but you need very fresh ingredients to pull it off. Leftovers, combined with chicken stock, make a wonderful soup.

ROASTED POTATOES

To roast potatoes, choose an all-purpose variety: the red potato (Nordland and Pontiac), the California White Rose (sometimes called Long White), or the yellow flesh potato (Yukon Gold, Yellow Finnish, and Bintje). Potatoes roasted in the oven don't take much time to prepare, don't need much attention while cooking, and they are always wonderful.

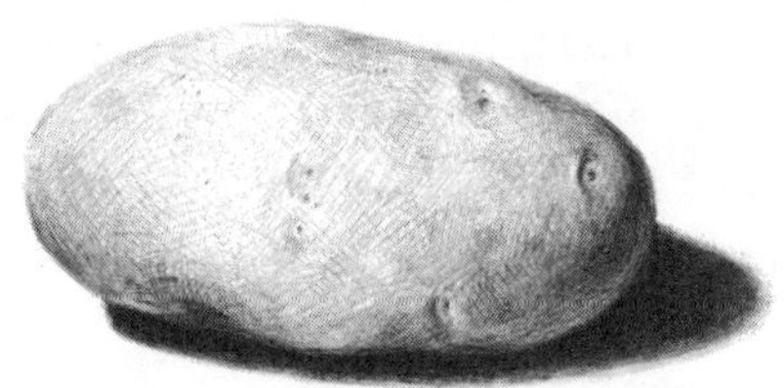

Roasted Potatoes Escoffier

I am sometimes asked to name my very favorite potato dish. The answer is Potatoes Escoffier, or the Danish variation that follows. Both dishes are easy to prepare and delicious. For Escoffier potatoes, as well as the Danish version, I peel the potatoes.

2 pounds Red Nordland, Red Pontiac, Yukon Gold, or White Rose potatoes, peeled and diced into 1-inch cubes (6 cups)
8 tablespoons (1 stick) butter or margarine, cut into small pieces
2 teaspoons salt

Preheat oven to 400 degrees.

Place the potatoes next to each other in a large cast-iron skillet. Pour in enough hot water to come one-quarter of the way up the potatoes. Distribute the butter or margarine evenly over the potatoes and sprinkle with salt. With a large spoon, combine water, butter, and potatoes.

Bake in the oven for 1 hour, or until the water has evaporated and the potatoes are lightly roasted.

Serves 4

Roasted Creamed Potatoes with Garlic

My friend Osa Sommemeyer, a superb cook, gave me this recipe from her native Denmark.

- 2 pounds Red Nordland, Red Pontiac, Yukon Gold, or White Rose potatoes, diced into 1-inch cubes (6 cups)
- 1 tablespoon butter
- 1 cup heavy cream
- 3 large garlic cloves, peeled and minced
- 1½ teaspoons salt
- Freshly ground pepper

Preheat the oven to 400 degrees.

Butter a 2-quart shallow baking dish. Toss together the potatoes, butter, cream, garlic, salt, and freshly ground pepper.

Bake on the middle shelf of the oven for 45 minutes, or until the potatoes are fork-tender and the cream has evaporated.

Serves 4

Potatoes Roasted in Olive Oil and Herbs

To roast potatoes in olive oil, use a light olive oil. A very expensive green olive oil will be too strong and will give a bitter taste to the potatoes. Substitute corn oil if you wish.

2 pounds White Rose, Yukon Gold, or Red Nordland or Pontiac potatoes, diced into 1½-inch cubes (6 cups)
⅓ cup light olive oil
1 tablespoon rosemary needles
Salt
Freshly ground pepper

Preheat oven to 400 degrees.

In a saucepan, cover the potatoes with cold salted water and bring to a boil. Turn off the heat and drain the potatoes.

In a roasting pan or large black iron skillet, heat the olive oil with the rosemary. Stir the potatoes into the hot fat and sprinkle with salt and pepper.

Place in the oven for 45 minutes, or until golden brown, stirring once in a while. Serve immediately.

NOTE: There are times when I roast a leg of lamb or a pork roast. I parboil whole unpeeled baby new potatoes (creamers), drain them, and put them under the rack of the roasting pan to cook and brown in the meat drippings instead of the olive oil used in the above recipe.

Serves 4

Roasted Potatoes Tatane

- 2 pounds Red Nordland, Red Pontiac, Yukon Gold, or White Rose potatoes, sliced lengthwise into thick french fries
- 6 tablespoons (3/4 stick) margarine
- Salt
- Freshly ground pepper

Preheat the oven to 400 degrees.

In a large pan, cover the potatoes with cold salted water. Bring to a boil and turn off the heat. Drain the potatoes.

Put the margarine in a roasting pan or a large black iron skillet and place in the oven for 3 minutes.

Toss the potatoes into the melted fat and sprinkle with salt and pepper.

Roast the potatoes on the middle shelf of the oven for 45 minutes, or until fork-tender, occasionally stirring them into the melted fat.

Serves 4

My aunt Tatane always cooked with margarine instead of butter like most thrifty housewives, not for health reasons but because it was cheaper. She peeled her potatoes (the French always peel their potatoes), but I don't. Choose potatoes of even size, weighing around 1/3 pound each.

8.
Fries

"Making french fries is the beginning of culinary art"

—Ali-Bab

In Europe, the Bintje variety,* a yellow flesh potato, is the most popular potato for making french fries. In the States, french fries are made with russet, the baking potato, or with mature Yukon Gold, an all-purpose yellow flesh potato.

Classic french fries are fried twice. The first frying can be done several hours before dinnertime and the second frying is always done at the last minute, barely taking 1 minute.

For french fries, choose large potatoes, about ½ lb each. Count at least 1 large potato per person. It's important that the size of the fries is even to avoid burning or undercooking.

There are gadgets that can shape the potatoes into the following common shapes for fries: *classic fries* (4 inches long and ¼ inch wide); *shoestring fries* (3 inches long and very skinny); and *matchstick fries* (about 1½ inches long and ⅛ inch thick). To cut classic and matchstick fries by hand: Cut the potatoes ¼ inch thick, stack a few slices at a time and cut ¼-inch-wide strips for the classic fries and ⅛-inch-wide strips for the matchstick fries.

Chips are cut into 1/16-inch-thick slices, *waffles* into ¼-inch-thick slices, and *Pommes soufflées* into ⅛-inch-thick slices.

*M. de Vries, a Dutch teacher at the beginning of this century, had a great hobby; he loved to interbreed potato seedlings to produce new varieties. Each new variety was baptized with the name of one of his nine children. He stopped having children but his passion for breeding potatoes continued. The tenth potato was named after one of his star pupils, young Bintje. The Bintje potato became famous—large, with yellow flesh, it's the all-purpose potato of Europe.

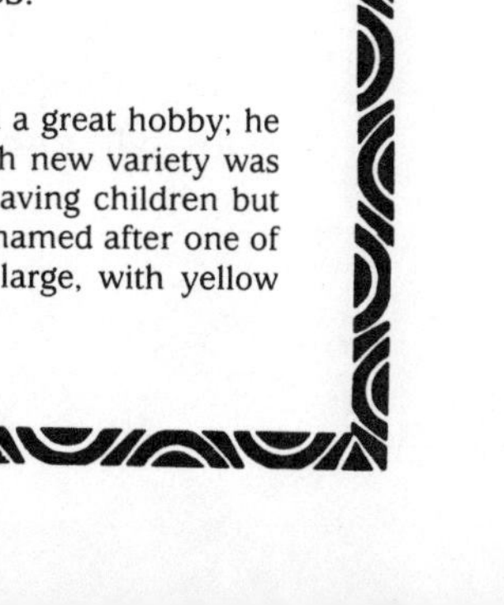

HOW TO DEEP-FRY

Don't refrigerate potatoes, especially for fries, because the starch is transformed into sugar when they are kept in cold storage, which means the sugar will burn in the hot fat before the potatoes are cooked through.

Wash the fries in warm water before deep-frying them to eliminate the starch at the surface, but don't leave them to soak for long, or they will become water-logged. It's important to dry thoroughly before frying. If the fries are still wet, the water, upon contact with the hot fat, will splatter, creating the danger of fire. *Always keep a lid next to you. In case of fire, turn off the heat and quickly cover the pan. Never use water; it will expand the fire rather than extinguish it.*

The frying oil must be tasteless, and must heat up to 375 degrees F without breaking down. Corn oil is highly recommended, but not olive oil. Shortening is also a favorite because its smoking point is well above 375 F.

After each use, strain the oil through cheesecloth or paper towels. Reserve in the refrigerator. Discard the oil after 5 or 6 uses.

For the first frying the oil is heated to 325 degrees, but once the potatoes are put in, the temperature drops to 250 degrees.

When the oil reaches 325 degrees, turn off the heat, just as a precaution against the oil bubbling over and causing a fire.

Slowly lower the fries into the hot oil, gently shaking the pan to disperse the fries, or use tongs to prevent them from clinging to each other (which should not happen if you have washed and dried them carefully). Turn the heat on and cook until the fries barely start to color, about 5 minutes. Drain and reserve in a colander, suspended over a bowl. Set aside until you are almost ready to eat.

Heat the oil for the second frying to 350 to 365 degrees and plunge the fries into the hot fat to brown instantly. Drain, sprinkle with salt, and serve immediately.

Classic French Fries

A 6-quart fryer 12 inches wide at the top, 9 inches wide at the bottom, and 4 inches high

2 pounds unpeeled (Yukon Gold or russet) potatoes
2 quarts plus 1 cup corn oil
Salt

Scrub the potatoes under cold water. Cut the potatoes into fries with a gadget for fries or with the french fry blade of the food processor. You should have about 8 cups of potatoes. (Discard any small pieces, which will burn.)

Put the potatoes in a large bowl filled with warm water and wash them thoroughly, drain, and pat very dry.

Heat the oil in the deep-fryer to 325 degrees; it will take about 4 minutes over high heat.

Turn off the heat (see page 146) and put in half the fries, lowering a ladleful of potatoes at a time into the hot oil. The oil will bubble instantly and expand to almost fill the pan.

Turn on the heat again and count about 5 minutes for the potatoes to render all their moisture and start cooking. At first, the fries will be limp, but as their moisture evaporates, they stiffen and start to color. When they are ready to color, transfer them to a wire basket clamped on a bowl.

Repeat with the second batch.

When almost ready for dinner, add 1 more cup of oil to the fryer. Heat to 350 to 365 degrees and drop all the fries in the pan without the basket (the basket takes too much space). They will turn golden brown within 1 minute. Drain in the frying basket. Sprinkle with salt and serve immediately.

Serves 4

Often when I eat fries, I make a meal of them, along with a tossed green salad. I don't peel the potatoes, I just scrub them clean.

French Fries Deep-Fried in Shortening

This is a home version of deep-frying. French cooks still fry in coconut oil extracted from the nut (copra); the oil is called Vegetaline *in French. Unfortunately, it is a highly saturated fat, but it has three great advantages: It does not get rancid as fast as oil; it is cheap; and the fries start in cold fat, a safer way to fry than the classic method of deep-frying in hot oil. I substituted shortening for Vegetaline, and tested both Vegetaline and shortening side by side. The shortening gave as good a result as Vegetaline.*

This technique is easier and less frightening than the technique for classic french fries. The cold shortening and potatoes are put in the deep-fryer at the same time. It takes about 20 minutes on high heat for the fat to reach 250 degrees and for the potatoes to fry. With this method, the starchier the potato, the better. I use the russet exclusively.

2 pounds russet potatoes (see page 145 for instructions on cutting and preparing)
One 3-pound can shortening
Salt

Put the shortening in a 6-quart deep-fryer, or a heavy-bottomed pan 10 inches wide and 5 inches high. Place the potatoes in the shortening. Turn the heat to high. The potatoes will turn lightly golden in about 25 minutes. Drain, sprinkle with salt, and serve immediately.

Strain the shortening back into its container and refrigerate until the next use. After using it twice, I add 1 cup of fresh shortening to replace what has been absorbed in the previous fryings.

Serves 4

Waffled Potatoes

1 pound russet potatoes, peeled and sliced ¼ inch thick (5 cups)

2 quarts plus 1 cup corn oil

Salt

Deep-fry the potatoes following the instructions on page 146 or page 147.

Serves 4

For waffled potatoes, slice the potatoes with a rippled-edge slicer, turning the potato ¼ way after each slice to create a grid pattern.

ON POTATO PUFFS (POMMES SOUFFLÉES)

August 26, 1837, is the official date of the accidental creation of pommes soufflées. King Louis Philippe and his queen, Amelie, were the honored guests at the Auberge de la Béarnaise, inaugurating a train line from Paris to Saint-Germain-en-Laye, a town about ten miles west of Paris. The menu listed filet mignon and french fries. Chef Collinet had it all organized, but everything went wrong. The train was late and Collinet had to let his fries cool for a second time. Finally, everybody settled down. Chef Collinet cooked his fries for the third time in hot oil, and miracle of miracle, they started to puff up like balloons. They were the hit of the party.

It sounds so simple, but unfortunately it's not so. How can a potato slice puff? Under heat, the starch in the potato changes into the chemical dextrin, a sticky substance that coagulates and forms an envelope that keeps steam in the potato slice. The steam makes the potato puff.

Two deep-fryers are necessary to make potato puffs, a large and a small, with the fat heated to different temperatures.

Pommes soufflées are made in three stages. The first cooks the potatoes, the next two make them puff. When they puff during the second stage, they immediately deflate when removed from the fat. During the third frying in very hot oil (365 degrees) they puff again and stay puffed—you hope! Potato puffs are capricious; some potato slices will puff, others will not. When I make them, about ⅔ puff, the others I eat like chips.

Choose potatoes of the same size. Peel and cut off the ends and sides to make perfect rectangles (I make matchstick potatoes with the discarded parts), then cut into even ⅛-inch-thick slices.

Potato Puffs

One 6-quart deep-fryer and one 4-quart deep-fryer

2 pounds Yukon Gold or russet potatoes, peeled and sliced 1/8 inch thick

3 quarts corn oil

Salt

Pour 2 quarts oil in the 6-quart deep-fryer. Heat to 325 degrees F.

Pour 1 quart oil in the 4-quart deep-fryer and heat the oil to 365 degrees.

Wash and pat very dry each potato slice. Plunge several potato slices, one at a time, into the large deep-fryer. Keep the slices from touching each other by very gently shaking the fryer.

Before they start to color, transfer the slices to the smaller fryer. They will puff up almost instantly, but this puffiness is not going to last. Transfer immediately to a wire basket fitted on a bowl. The potatoes will shrivel. (The procedure can be done to this point several hours before serving.)

Add the oil from the small deep-fryer to the big one. Heat to 365 degrees F. Plunge the basket with the potatoes into the hot oil. Shake the basket to dislodge the potatoes from each other. As soon as they come back to the surface, they will puff and will stay puffed, with luck.

Remove the basket from the oil and shake it over a bowl to drain the potatoes completely. Spread them on a cloth towel. Sprinkle with salt and serve.

Serves 4

Potato Chips

As I do with french fries, I make a meal of chips and a tossed salad. Each serving of chips is about 400 calories, not as bad as one would think. How did I get 400 calories per serving? 2 pounds of potatoes contain 800 calories, and the corn oil contributes 800 calories (½ cup or 8 tablespoons were absorbed by the potatoes, and 1 tablespoon of oil is 100 calories).

One 6-quart deep-fryer, 12 inches wide at the top, 9 inches wide at the bottom, and 4 inches high

2 pounds unpeeled russet or Yukon Gold potatoes, sliced 1/16 inch thick (8 cups)
2 quarts corn oil
Salt

Wash the potato slices in warm water, drain, and pat dry. Place potato slices next to each other on a large dish towel, cover with another dish towel, and dry the slices evenly.

Heat the oil to 325 degrees. Put half the slices in the fryer, taking a small ladleful at a time and lowering them into the hot fat. Count about 5 minutes for the potatoes to disgorge their moisture and to start cooking. At first the slices of potatoes will be limp, but as the moisture evaporates, they will stiffen. Do not let them brown at all. Remove to a wire basket clamped over a large bowl.

Bring the fat back to 325 degrees and deep-fry the remaining slices of potatoes. Transfer them to the wire basket.

When ready to eat, heat the oil to 365 degrees. Plunge the fries in the hot oil for 45 seconds, or until golden.

Transfer again in the wire basket to drain any fat still clinging to the chips. Put in a large serving platter, sprinkle with salt, and serve immediately.

Serves 4

Potato Birds' Nests

1 pound Yukon Gold or russet potatoes, peeled and shredded into matchsticks (4 cups)
3 quarts corn oil
Salt

Line the inside of the large ladle with ½ cup shredded potatoes; line a second layer across the bottom layer with another ½ cup of potatoes. Place the smaller ladle inside the larger ladle over the potatoes and clamp the 2 together. With a pair of scissors, cut off the straggly potato shreds that stick out of the ladles.

Heat the oil to 300 degrees in a 10-quart stockpot or any pan with very high sides. Plunge the potatoes into the hot fat and hook the ladles to the side of the stock pot. Fry about 5 minutes, but do not let the potatoes color. Drain.

Heat the oil to 350 degrees and fry the nest a second time for 1 minute, or until the nest is golden brown (be very careful not to burn them at this point).

Remove the clamps and the larger ladle (it will come out easily), and hit the smaller ladle against the side of a bowl to loosen the potato nest. Salt and keep warm until all birds' nests are fried.

Serve filled with potato puffs, chips, or waffled potatoes.

Serves 4

When you have time to play in the kitchen, it's fun to make birds' nests, but you need a special tool for them: 2 wire ladles, the smaller nesting into the larger and held together by 2 clamps. There are 3 sizes of ladle sets. I use the middle-sized set with the larger ladle measuring 5 inches in diameter at the top and the smaller one measuring 4 inches. If you are planning to make several birds' nests at a time, it's worth buying more than one set of ladles; otherwise, deep-fry 1 nest, unmold it, and keep it warm while you fry the next.

I use my stockpot to fry the nests. The handles of the ladles are long and hook onto the side of the pot, freeing the cook from holding the nests for 5 or 6 minutes.

The potatoes are grated into matchsticks (the food processor grater is perfect).

This peasant version of french fries is deep-fried twice with onions. Fried in batches, the potatoes can wait to be re-fried in a minute just before dinner.

Country Fried Potatoes with Onions

One 6-quart deep-fryer, 12 inches wide at the top and 4 inches deep

3 pounds Yukon Gold or russet potatoes, peeled and cut into ½-inch cubes (8 cups)
2 quarts corn oil
6 white onions, peeled and quartered
Salt

Wash the potato cubes in cold water. Drain well and pat dry in towels.

Heat the oil to 325 degrees. Deep-fry in 2 batches, lowering the potatoes slowly into the hot fat, a ladleful at a time. Fry for 15 minutes, stirring the potatoes in the fat occasionally.

Add half of the onions and continue deep-frying. Lower the heat (to prevent the onions from burning) and fry for about 10 to 15 more minutes or until the potatoes are just ready to brown.

With a wire skimmer, transfer the potatoes and onions to a big strainer placed over a bowl. Repeat with the next batch of potatoes and onions.

At dinnertime, reheat the oil to 350 degrees and deep-fry all the potatoes and onions together until crisp (about 1 minute).

Strain, sprinkle with salt at the last minute, and serve immediately.

Serves 6

Potato Croquettes

One 6-quart deep-fryer, 12 inches wide at the top and 4 inches deep

2 quarts corn oil
2 pounds Yukon Gold or russet potatoes, peeled and finely shredded into matchsticks (6 cups)
6 ounces Gruyère, grated (2 cups)
About 1/3 cup flour, depending on the moisture in the potatoes, plus flour for dredging the croquettes
Salt

Heat the corn oil to 325 degrees.

Mix the shredded potatoes with cheese and flour.

Flour your hands and make patties, 3 inches wide and 1 inch thick. Put as many as you can in the hot fat and fry both sides until golden, about 4 or 5 minutes. Drain carefully and put in a wire basket over a bowl.

Sprinkle the croquettes with salt and serve immediately.

Serves 6

These potato croquettes are delicious but a little messy to make.

Pommes à la Dunkerquoise

BOILED AND FRIED POTATOES

In northern France, near Dunkirk, housewives boil the potatoes before frying them at the last minute. The fries taste lighter with this technique.

One 6-quart deep-fryer, 12 inches wide at the top and 4 inches deep

2 pounds Yukon Gold or russet potatoes, peeled and cut into ½-inch cubes (6 cups)
2 quarts corn oil
Salt

In a large saucepan, cover the potatoes with cold salted water and bring to a boil. Partially cover and cook for 15 minutes, or until almost tender. Drain and set aside to cool.

Pat the potatoes dry on paper towels. They must be absolutely dry before frying. (Recipe can be made ahead to this point.)

When ready to serve, heat the corn oil to 325 degrees. Turn off the heat and lower the potatoes into the hot fat, a spoonful at a time. When the oil surface stops bubbling furiously, turn on the heat and fry the potatoes until golden brown.

Drain and sprinkle with salt. Serve immediately.

Serves 4

Napoleons of Potato Chips

2 pounds Yukon Gold or russet potatoes, 1 pound peeled and diced into 1-inch cubes (3 cups); the other pound peeled and sliced
$^{1}/_{16}$ inch thick (2 cups)
4 strips bacon
½ to ¾ cup heavy cream
1 teaspoon salt
Freshly ground pepper
3 tablespoons minced chives
8 tablespoons (1 stick) clarified butter (see page 6 for clarifying butter)

I learned to make these napoleons in the kitchen of Taillevent, one of the most elegant restaurants in Paris.

In a large pan, cover the cubed potatoes with cold salted water and bring to a boil. Partially cover and cook for 15 to 20 minutes, or until tender.

Cook the bacon in a skillet over moderate heat until crisp and brown, about 5 minutes. Drain on paper towels and crumble.

Drain the cooked potatoes. Mash with a potato masher, ricer, or through a strainer into the cooking pan. Over medium heat, beat in the cream, salt and pepper. If the mixture is too stiff, beat in up to ¼ cup more cream.

Fold in the bacon, and 2 tablespoons chives. Put the pan of potatoes in a pan of simmering water. Cover the potatoes with foil and stir occasionally.

For the chips, wash the potato slices, drain, and pat very dry. Heat the clarified butter and fry the chips in batches, for 3 minutes per batch, or until golden brown.

Transfer them with a slotted spoon to a baking sheet. Sprinkle lightly with salt. Keep them warm on top of the mashed potato bowl in the water bath until ready to eat them.

For the presentation: Put 1 tablespoon of mashed potatoes on each plate, and top with a potato chip. Make 2 more layers, ending with a potato chip. Garnish with the remaining chives.

At Taillevent, these wonderful "millefeuilles" are presented as a side dish for main meat courses.

Serves 6

9.
Gratins and Scalloped Potatoes

Potato gratins are baked in wide, shallow baking pans. This is generally a dish that cooks slowly in the oven for a long time. The potatoes are sliced and cooked in a liquid, such as milk, cream, water, beer, wine, or broth. They can be cooked with other vegetables as well. The top of the gratin will brown from the long baking time in the oven. The American scalloped potato is what the French call a gratin, because the potatoes are sliced, baked in a traditional shallow baking dish, and the top develops a light crust tinged with gold.

The word *gratin* comes from the French verb *gratter*, which means to scrape. In cooking terms, gratin refers both to the dish prepared and the pan in which it is cooked. *Gratiné* or *au gratin* is a description of the crust formed by sprinkling bread crumbs or cheese over food and heating under a broiler. (Figuratively, "le gratin" is the uppercrust of society.)

The quality of the potato is important for an excellent gratin, and it is also a touchy subject. I know cooks and chefs who swear by the russet potato, the baking potato. I did, too, for many years, but lately I've switched to buying the all-purpose potato for gratins. It retains a firm texture, while the baking potato gives a more pasty texture. In my cooking classes, I have simultaneously tested gratins made with the russet and with the Yukon Gold. There wasn't universal agreement, but the majority preferred the gratins made with the Yukon Gold potato. The California White Rose potato or the Eastern potato will also make excellent gratins.

It is important to slice the potatoes evenly, between 1/8 inch and 1/16 inch thick, lengthwise or crosswise, with a chef's knife, a cleaver, or with the 3-millimeter blade of a food processor. Profes-

sionals slice with a mandoline, a heavy stainless steel contraption that slices, juliennes, and cuts french fries in a variety of thicknesses.

Should the raw potato slices be rinsed or not before assembling the gratin? Some say yes, some say no. In the following recipes, I did not rinse the potatoes because I wanted the starch to act as a binder with the liquid in the gratin.

The size of the gratin (baking) pan is important; the wider the surface, the more area to brown. The pan should be shallow and only ¾ full, allowing the liquid to bubble without spilling over. For 2 pounds of unpeeled potatoes, I use a pan approximately 14 by 8 by 2 inches.

Gratins are the perfect accompaniment to a meat course, especially lamb roast. (Elizabeth David likes to eat hers for a first course.) When gratins are combined with fish or bacon, they can become a meal.

Potato Gratin with Pistou

3 tablespoons olive oil
2 pounds Yukon Gold, White Rose, or russet potatoes, peeled and sliced 1/8 inch to 1/16 inch thick (6 cups)
1 1/2 teaspoons salt
Freshly ground pepper
Pistou (page 32)
2 medium onions, peeled and thinly sliced

Preheat the oven to 325 degrees.

Oil a 2-quart rectangular or oval baking dish 14 by 8 by 2 and layer half the potatoes at the bottom of it. Season with 1/2 teaspoon salt and freshly ground pepper. Spread half the pistou in the pan and put the onion slices on top. Layer on the last of the potatoes, salt, and pepper. Spread in the remaining pistou and dribble 2 tablespoons olive oil on top.

Bake in the middle of the oven for 1 1/2 to 2 hours, or until the potatoes are tender; loosely cover the top with foil if the gratin browns too fast.

Serves 6

Fresh basil is called pistou in Provence, but it also means a mixture of basil, tomatoes, garlic, and cheese.

Sorrel is a perennial green. Its acidic nature marries beautifully with any meat or vegetable delicate in flavor; for instance, try a sorrel sauce over fish or veal. Baked with potatoes, it is delectable. I ate this gratin of potatoes and creamed sorrel one summer day at Richard Olney's lovely place in southern France.

Potato Gratin with Sorrel

One 2-quart rectangular or oval baking dish 14 by 8 by 2 inches

2 pounds Yukon Gold, White Rose, or russet potatoes, peeled and sliced 1/8 inch to 1/16 inch thick (6 cups)
3 medium onions, peeled and thinly sliced
1 1/2 teaspoons salt
3 tablespoons butter or margarine
1/2 pound sorrel, stems removed, coarsely chopped (6 cups)
1 cup heavy cream
1 garlic clove, peeled and minced

Put the potato and onion slices in a saucepan and pour in 2 cups of water. Add 1 teaspoon of the salt. Bring to a boil, shaking the pan to prevent the vegetables from sticking to the bottom. Turn off the heat at the boil. Drain the potatoes and onions but reserve the cooking liquid for later.

Melt 2 tablespoons of the butter or margarine in a skillet, add the sorrel, and cook for 2 minutes, wilting it into a purée. Mix in the cream and the remaining 1/2 teaspoon salt. Cook for 3 minutes or longer, stirring occasionally, until the mixture thickens.

Preheat the oven to 325 degrees.

Rub the baking dish with the remaining 1 tablespoon butter or margarine and scatter in the minced garlic.

Put the potatoes and onions in the baking dish; pour in the cooking liquid and spread the creamy sorrel on top.

Bake in the middle shelf of the oven for 1 to 1 1/2 hours, or until the potatoes are fork-tender and the top is golden brown.

Serves 6

Potato Gratin with Watercress

Substitute 6 cups of watercress leaves for the sorrel in the preceding recipe.

The day I planned to teach scalloped potatoes with sorrel in Phoenix, Arizona, I had the nasty surprise of discovering that a pound of sorrel cost $12. I was flabbergasted; sorrel grows like a weed! Sherri Springer, a cooking teacher in Arizona who was in my class, suggested watercress instead, for those who could not grow their own sorrel and did not want to pay a fortune. It was a great idea.

Potato Gratin with Peppers, Onions, and Tomatoes

- 1/3 cup olive oil
- 4 garlic cloves, peeled and minced
- 2 pounds Yukon Gold, White Rose, or russet potatoes, peeled and sliced 1/8 inch to 1/16 inch thick (6 cups)
- 1 yellow pepper, sliced 1/8 inch thick
- 1 red pepper, sliced 1/8 inch thick
- 3 large tomatoes, sliced 1/8 inch thick
- 1 Spanish onion, peeled and sliced 1/8 inch thick
- 1 1/2 teaspoons salt
- Freshly ground pepper
- 2 tablespoons fresh oregano

Preheat the oven to 325 degrees.

Dribble 1 tablespoon olive oil into a 2-quart rectangular or oval baking dish 14 by 8 by 2 and scatter 1/4 of the minced garlic over the bottom of the pan.

Arrange the vegetables in layers, starting with potatoes and peppers, finishing with tomatoes and onion. Sprinkle salt, freshly ground pepper, garlic, and oregano between each layer.

Pour the remaining olive oil over the surface and bake in the oven for 1 1/2 hours, or until fork-tender.

Serves 6

Gratin Dauphinois

No one agrees on what makes an authentic gratin dauphinois. According to Curnonsky ("the gourmet of all gourmets"), it contains no eggs or cheese. He thought that eggs dried out the gratin and that the cheese hid the taste of the potatoes. He wanted just potatoes with cream and a hint of garlic.

Another dispute raging among Dauphinois maniacs is the right thickness of the potato slices. Should the potatoes be paper-thin, less than 1/16 inch, or should they be cut between 1/8 inch and 1/16 inch? In rural kitchens in the Dauphiné or elsewhere, the potatoes are sliced thicker than in kitchens of restaurants. Chefs slice potatoes ultrathin with a professional mandoline, whereas many homemakers slice them with a knife. To tell the truth, it does not matter. The gratins are excellent in all shapes and forms. After all, what is better than cream, garlic, and butter combined with potatoes?

1 large garlic clove, peeled and minced
2 pounds Yukon Gold or russet potatoes, peeled and sliced 1/8 inch to 1/16 inch thick (6 cups)
1 1/2 teaspoons salt
1 1/3 cups half and half
1 tablespoon cold butter
1/3 cup heavy cream

Preheat the oven to 325 degrees. Butter a 2-quart rectangular or oval dish 14 by 8 by 2 inches. Scatter the minced garlic in the dish.

Overlap 3 layers of potatoes in the pan, sprinkling salt between each layer. Dribble in the half and half, barely covering them. Dot the top with butter.

Bake in the middle of the oven for 45 minutes. Pour the heavy cream on top of the potatoes and tilt the pan to baste the top layer. Bake for 45 minutes more, or until golden brown.

Serves 4 to 6

American Scalloped Potatoes

2 tablespoons flour
1 1/2 teaspoons salt
1/8 teaspoon freshly ground pepper
2 pounds Yukon Gold, Superior, or White Rose potatoes, peeled and sliced 1/8 inch to 1/16 inch thick (6 cups)
2 tablespoons butter
2 cups milk

Recipes for scalloped potatoes in the United States and Canada call for flour between the layers of potatoes. That is the chief difference between American scalloped potatoes and gratin dauphinois. American boiling potatoes are moister than European varieties and the flour is needed to soak up the liquid.

Preheat the oven to 350 degrees. Butter a 2-quart rectangular or oval baking dish 14 by 8 by 2 inches.

Combine the flour, salt, and pepper. Overlap 1/3 of the potato slices in the pan. Sprinkle with half the flour mixture and dot with 1 tablespoon butter. Add a second layer of potatoes, sprinkle over the last of the flour mixture, and dot with the remaining butter. Cover with the last layer of potatoes. Pour milk over the top.

Cover with aluminum foil and bake in the middle of the oven for 45 minutes. Reduce the temperature to 325 degrees, uncover, and continue baking for another 45 minutes, or until the top is tinged with gold.

Serves 6

Valdrome, the French village where my ancestors came from, situated astride the Dauphine and the Provence regions, is famous for this potato gratin. There, the gratin is called gratin dauphinois even though it has no cream in it. Cooking in Valdrome is done on or inside wood-burning stoves fueled with dried broom and walnut wood. Meats and fowl are braised very slowly for hours in a dutch oven on top of the stove, making wonderful meat drippings for gratins. The potatoes are sautéed in the meat drippings with onions, garlic, and thyme, then covered with a local red wine and slowly braised in the oven for 2 or 3 hours where the dish develops a crusty top.

Potato Gratin in Red Wine

- **1/4 cup chicken fat or drippings from a roast**
- **2 pounds Yukon Gold, White Rose, or russet potatoes, peeled and sliced 1/8 inch to 1/16 inch thick (6 cups)**
- **1 large onion, peeled and chopped**
- **2 garlic cloves, peeled and minced**
- **1 1/2 teaspoons salt**
- **1 teaspoon dried thyme**
- **1 cup red wine**
- **1 bay leaf**
- **1 tablespoon olive oil**

Preheat the oven to 325 degrees.

In a large skillet, melt the chicken fat or meat drippings. Add half the potatoes, onion, and garlic. Shaking the skillet all the while, stir-fry for several minutes until the edges of the potatoes start to color. Season with 1 teaspoon salt and 1/2 teaspoon thyme. Mix well and transfer to a 2-quart rectangular or oval baking dish. Sauté the remaining potatoes, onion, and garlic. Season with salt and thyme and transfer to the baking dish.

Pour the wine and 1/2 cup water over the potatoes. Crumble a bay leaf on top and dribble on the olive oil. Bake for 1 1/2 hours, or until golden brown.

Serves 6

Potato Gratin with Blue Cheese

4 ounces blue cheese
1/2 cup heavy cream
2 pounds Yukon Gold, White Rose, or russet potatoes, peeled and sliced 1/8 inch to 1/16 inch thick (6 cups)
1 1/2 teaspoons salt
Freshly ground pepper
2 cups milk
1 1/2 tablespoons unsalted butter

Every region of France has it own potato gratin, and this one is from the Auvergne in central France, famous for its cheeses. The gratin is best made with bleu d'Auvergne.

Preheat oven to 350 degrees. Butter a 2-quart rectangular or oval baking dish 14 by 8 by 2 inches.

Process the cheese and cream in a food processor for 10 seconds.

Overlap 1/3 of the potato slices in 1 layer in the pan. Sprinkle on 1 teaspoon salt and some freshly ground pepper, and cover with half the cheese mixture. Layer the remaining potato slices on top, cover with the rest of the cheese mixture, and pour over the milk. Dot with shavings of butter.

Bake in the middle shelf of the oven for 1 1/2 hours, or until golden brown.

Serves 6

Potato Gratin with Onions and Beer

Belgians cook with beer; this is their version of a potato gratin.

- 2 pounds Yukon Gold, White Rose, or russet potatoes, peeled and sliced 1/16 inch thick (6 cups)
- 1 cup beer
- 3 tablespoons butter or margarine
- 4 cups coarsely chopped onions
- 1 1/2 teaspoons salt
- Freshly ground pepper
- 1 cup grated Gruyère

In a large bowl, toss the potatoes with the beer.

Melt 2 tablespoons of the butter or margarine in a dutch oven, add the chopped onions, sprinkle with 1/2 teaspoon salt and freshly ground pepper, and stir. Cover and simmer slowly for 15 minutes, checking that the onions do not burn.

Preheat the oven to 350 degrees. Butter a 2-quart rectangular or oval baking dish 14 by 8 by 2 inches.

Overlap 1/3 of the potato slices in 1 layer, season with 1/2 teaspoon salt and freshly ground pepper. Sprinkle on 1/3 cup Gruyère and half the braised onions. Continue with 2 more layer, ending with cheese. (There will be only 2 layers of onions.) Pour the beer over the potatoes and dot the top with the remaining butter.

Bake on the middle shelf of the oven for 1 1/2 hours.

Serves 6

Gratin Savoyard

2 pounds Yukon Gold, White Rose, or russet potatoes, peeled and sliced 1/16 inch thick (6 cups)
1 1/2 teaspoons salt
Freshly ground pepper
2 cups grated Gruyère
4 tablespoons (1/2 stick) unsalted butter or margarine
1 cup chicken stock

Preheat the oven to 425 degrees. Butter a 2-quart rectangular or oval baking dish 14 by 8 by 2 inches.

Overlap 1/3 of the potato slices in 1 layer in the dish. Sprinkle with 1/2 teaspoon salt, freshly ground pepper, and 1/3 of the cheese; dot with shavings of butter. Repeat with 2 more layers of potatoes, cheese, butter, and seasoning. Pour the chicken stock over the potatoes.

Bake in the middle of the oven for 1/2 hour. Lower the temperature to 350 degrees and tilt the pan to baste the top layer of potatoes with the stock in the pan. Bake for 1/2 hour more, or until golden brown.

Serves 6

In Savoie, in the French Alps, the gratin of potatoes is cooked with homemade chicken stock.

When you feel like celebrating, splurge with potatoes and truffles. In this dish, instead of slicing the potatoes, I shred them coarsely because I find that shredded potatoes absorb the aroma of the truffles better than sliced ones.

I give a poor man's version here with just 1½ ounces of canned truffles, but go right ahead if you feel like putting more truffles in the dish.

Potato Gratin with Truffles

2 pounds Yukon Gold, White Rose, or russet potatoes, peeled and grated medium coarse in a mouli-julienne or food processor (8 cups)
4 garlic cloves, peeled and minced
One 1½-ounce can truffles, diced
1½ teaspoons salt
Freshly ground pepper
6 tablespoons butter or margarine

Preheat the oven to 400 degrees. Butter a 2-quart rectangular or oval baking dish 14 by 8 by 2 inches.

Plunge the grated potatoes in a large bowl of cold water. Drain and pat dry.

Mix the garlic, truffles, salt, and freshly ground pepper with the potatoes. Make 3 piles.

Melt 2 tablespoons butter or margarine in a nonstick skillet over high heat.

When the fat sizzles, stir in 1 batch of potatoes and sauté for 2 minutes. Transfer the potatoes to the prepared baking dish and sauté the next 2 batches of potatoes, adding butter or margarine for each batch.

Dribble the truffle juice over the top of the potatoes and dot the surface with 1 tablespoon butter or margarine.

Bake in the middle shelf of the oven for 30 minutes, or until the potatoes are tender and the top is golden.

Serves 6

Potato Gratin with Morels

1 ounce dried morels

Soak the morels for 1 hour in 1 cup warm water. Drain in a paper-lined strainer. Reserve and set aside the juice. Wash the morels once more under running cold water to get rid of any grit. Chop the morels coarsely.

Proceed with the preceding potato gratin recipe, substituting morels for truffles.

Boil the morel liquid down to ½ cup. Sprinkle 1 tablespoon of the morel liquid over the gratin just before baking it. Reserve the remaining morel liquid for basting a roast, or freeze it.

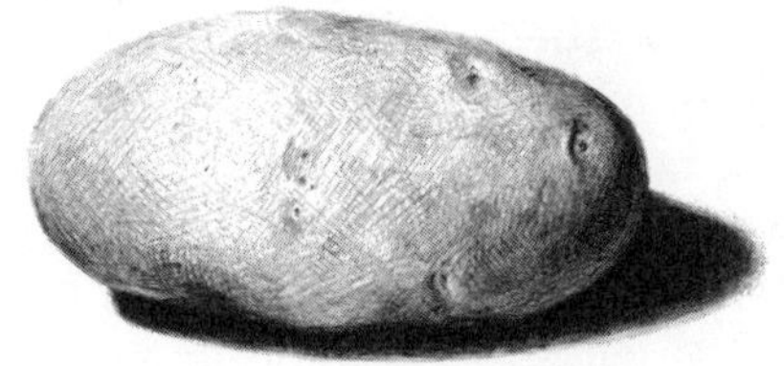

This gratin with morels is excellent with a veal roast.

The 3 following gratins can be served as a main dish, with a tossed green salad.

Jansson's Temptation

JANZON'S FRESTELSE

2 pounds Yukon Gold, White Rose, or russet potatoes, peeled and grated medium coarse in the mouli-julienne or food processor (8 cups)
1 teaspoon salt
Freshly ground pepper
16 anchovy fillets, washed, dried, and cut in half (about two 2½-ounce cans), or 8 to 10 Swedish anchovy sprats (see Note)
3 medium onions, peeled and thinly sliced (about 3 cups)
1½ cups heavy cream
5 tablespoons fresh breadcrumbs

Preheat the oven to 400 degrees.

Place the grated potatoes in a large bowl of cold water. Drain and pat dry. In a large bowl, toss the potatoes, salt, and freshly ground pepper with your hands.

Smear the bottom of a 2-quart rectangular or oval gratin pan with 1 teaspoon oil from the anchovy can. Spread half the grated potatoes in the pan. Layer over the anchovy fillets and the onion slices. Cover with the remaining potatoes and pour on the cream. Sprinkle with breadcrumbs and dribble on the remaining oil from the anchovies.

Bake for 1 hour, or until the gratin is golden brown.

There are many stories about how Jansson's temptation got its name, writes Dale Brown in The Cooking of Scandinavia. *"The dish is named after Erik Janson, the nineteenth century Swedish religious zealot and self-appointed prophet who took his disciples to America and founded a colony called Bishop Hill in Illinois. Although adamantly opposed to the pleasures of the flesh, one day Janson found himself so sorely tempted by this crusty dish that he threw over his principles to eat some—in secret of course. He was caught in the act by a disillusioned follower. The story is a good one but undoubtedly apocryphal. Janson and Jansson are not even spelled the same way."*

Less amusing but perhaps truer to the origin of the dish is the story I read in the English cookbook, In Praise of Potatoes *by Lindsey Benham. Adolf Janzon, son of a fisherman, became a famous opera singer, known*

NOTE: Canned Swedish anchovy fillets are smelts pickled in salt, spices, and sugar. If anchovy sprats are available, remove them from the can and skin and bone the sprats to produce 16 to 20 fillets. Cut each fillet in half. And substitute olive oil for the oil in the regular canned anchovies.

Serves 4

Potato Gratin with Bacon

1 teaspoon olive oil
2 pounds Yukon Gold, White Rose, or russet potatoes, peeled and sliced 1/8 inch to 1/16 inch thick (6 cups)
1 1/2 teaspoons salt
Freshly ground pepper
2 garlic cloves, peeled and minced
1/2 pound bacon (10 slices)
1 cup chicken broth or water

Preheat the oven to 325 degrees. Oil a 2-quart rectangular or oval baking dish 14 by 8 by 2 inches.

Overlap half the potatoes in 1 layer in the baking dish. Sprinkle with 1/2 teaspoon salt, freshly ground pepper, and the minced garlic. Overlap the remaining potatoes, seasoning with salt and freshly ground pepper. Cover the potatoes with the bacon slices. Pour 1 cup chicken broth or water over the bacon.

Bake in the middle of the oven for 1 1/2 hours, until the potatoes are tender and the top is lightly browned.

Serves 4

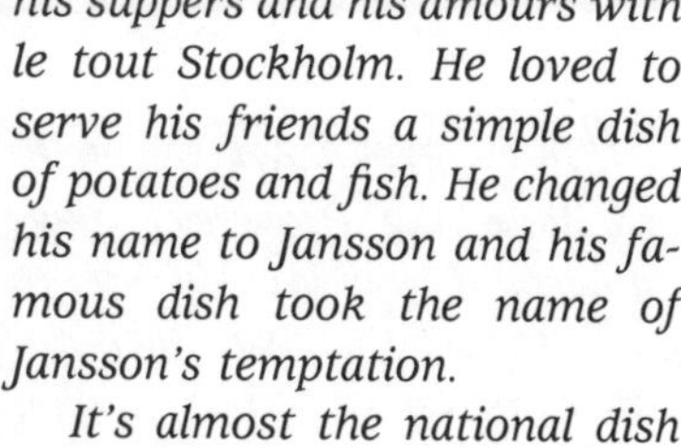

not only for his voice, but for his suppers and his amours with le tout Stockholm. He loved to serve his friends a simple dish of potatoes and fish. He changed his name to Jansson and his famous dish took the name of Jansson's temptation.

It's almost the national dish of Sweden. The host serves it as the party breaks up so the guests have something warm and strong in their stomachs against the cold.

This tasty peasant fare is best made with a bacon that is not too heavily smoked and not too fatty, but do not substitute Canadian; it is too dry for this dish.

You either love or hate brandade, the Provençal mayonnaise. If you love it, you're going to love this dish. I serve it either as an appetizer, giving small portions, or as a main dish with watercress. When buying salt cod, be sure it has not been shelved for months, as it develops a strong flavor. Canadian fisheries sell salt cod under its Portuguese name, bacalao.

Gratin of Mashed Potatoes and Brandade

FOR THE BRANDADE:

- 8 ounces salt cod
- 2 garlic cloves, peeled and coarsely chopped
- 2/3 cup olive oil, heated
- 1/2 cup boiling milk
- 1/4 cup heavy cream, heated

FOR THE MASHED POTATOES:

- 2 pounds russet potatoes, peeled and cut into 2-inch cubes (5 cups)
- 1 cup milk, scalded
- 5 tablespoons unsalted butter or margarine, at room temperature
- Salt
- Freshly ground pepper

Put the salt cod in a large bowl of cold water in the sink under a trickling of running water for 1 to 2 hours. Keep refrigerated overnight in cold water.

Drain the salt cod and cover it with cold water in a pan. Bring to a near boil and poach for 20 minutes in water that just quivers.

Drain the cod and combine it with the garlic in the bowl of a food processor fitted with the metal blade. Process until smooth, about 30 seconds, scraping down the work bowl as necessary. With the motor running, drizzle the hot oil and milk alternately through the feed tube, scraping down the work bowl as necessary.

Reheat in a small saucepan over low heat, gradually stirring in the cream.

In a saucepan, cover the potatoes with cold salted water and bring to a boil. Partially cover and cook for 20 minutes, or until the potatoes are tender.

Drain the potatoes and mash them in the cooking pan with an

old-fashioned potato masher, or through a ricer or strainer back into the pan. Gradually pour in the milk.

Over medium heat, with a wooden spoon beat 4 tablespoons butter or margarine, tablespoon by tablespoon, into the potatoes.

Preheat the oven to 300 degrees. Butter a 1½-quart rectangular or oval dish (12 by 8 by 2), a 6-cup soufflé mold, or twelve ½-cup ramekins.

Combine the brandade and the mashed potatoes; season with salt and freshly ground pepper to taste. Put in the prepared dish or ramekins. Dot the surface with shavings of the remaining butter and reheat in the oven for about 15 minutes.

Set the broiler on high and gratiné the top for 1 minute.

Serves 6 as a main course, 12 as an appetizer

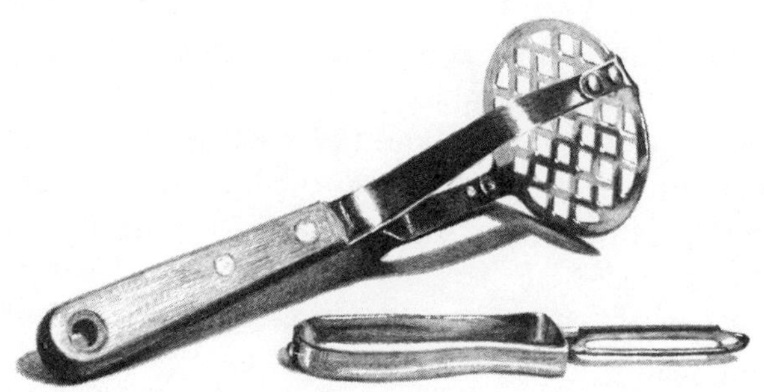

Gratin of Mashed Potatoes and a Ragout of Mussels

Choose your favorite mashed potato recipe to accompany the ragout of mussels. I like to combine it with colcannon, the Irish mashed potatoes speckled with kale; it looks very colorful and tastes wonderful. Just be sure not to exceed 1 pound of mashed potatoes for 2 pounds mussels; with too much mashed potatoes, the mussels get lost in the dish.

2 pounds mussels
2 tablespoons butter
1 large onion, peeled and minced
1 tablespoon flour
1 cup white wine
Salt
½ recipe Colcannon (page 108)
1 cup grated Gruyère

Scrub the mussels clean. Keep them in a bowl of cold water.

Drain the mussels and put them in a large kettle with ½ cup water, cover, and steam over medium heat, shaking the pan occasionally, until the mussels open (about 3 minutes).

Discard the shells and reserve the mussels. Strain the mussel liquid through cheesecloth. Reserve.

In a large skillet, melt the butter. Add the onion and cook until wilted but not browned. Sprinkle flour over the onion and mix thoroughly. Pour in the mussel liquid and white wine and whisk until smooth. Cook for 15 minutes over medium heat, or until the sauce becomes creamy. Taste and add salt if necessary. Add the mussels and mix well.

Preheat the oven to 350 degrees. Butter a 2-quart oval or rectangular baking dish.

Spread the mashed potatoes at the bottom of the buttered pan. Cover with the mussels and sauce. Sprinkle with cheese and bake for 15 minutes.

To gratiné, set the broiler on high and place the gratin 5 inches from the heat source for 1 minute.

Serves 6

Barbecued Scalloped Potatoes

- 1 pound bacon slices (about 20), cut in half crosswise
- 2 pounds unpeeled Yukon Gold, White Rose, or russet potatoes, sliced 1/8 inch to 1/16 inch thick (6 cups)
- 1 teaspoon salt
- Freshly ground pepper
- 3 tablespoons butter or margarine
- 10 ounces sharp Cheddar, grated (2 1/2 cups)
- 1 cup sour cream
- 3 tablespoons minced chives

Prepare the barbecue.

Layer 1/3 of the bacon at the bottom of an 11- by 8- by 1-inch foil broiler pan and spread over the bacon 2 layers of potatoes, sprinkling salt and pepper between the layers. Add small pieces of butter on every fifth potato slice, and in between put 1/3 of the cheese. Spread on 1/3 of the sour cream mixed with the chives. Repeat the layers of bacon, potatoes, butter, cheese, finishing with sour cream.

Cover the pan with foil and crimp the foil tightly around the edges.

Put over hot coals on a grill, cover, and bake for 30-40 minutes or until potatoes are fork-tender.

Cut slits at the bottom of the pan and drain the fat. Serve immediately.

Serves 4 to 6

I found a tearsheet from an old magazine (perhaps from the 1940s) with a recipe for barbecued scalloped potatoes in an ad for Meyer's butter. The recipe is given step by step with the picture of crew-cut Jim Bellamy, Meyer's adman, cooking his scalloped potatoes for Shirley Bennett, a potential buyer of Meyer's butter. The ad reads: "Start with aluminum foil. Lay down a layer of bacon and cover with 2 layers of potatoes, sliced about 1/8 inch. Next place patties of Meyer's butter on about every fifth potato slice. Sprinkle with salt and pepper. Could you use X brand butter? Perhaps, but it wouldn't be Genuine Potatoes Bellamy. Add slices of sharp Cheddar cheese between the patties of Meyer's butter. Then top it all with a liberal covering of Meyer's sour cream and chives. Start all over again with a layer of bacon etc. Make 3 complete layers. Seal the foil. Place over hot coals for 45 minutes. Punch a hole in the foil, drain the grease and serve. Wow!"

10. Potato Dumplings and Gnocchi

The better the cook, the lighter the dumpling. When people respond to the mention of pierogi or gnocchi with a gesture like puffing cheeks or the comment "heavy as lead," they reveal they've never eaten the real thing.

But I must admit, from the sample of these dishes I have eaten in restaurants, it is understandable why dumplings are so maligned; they are generally inedible. Well-made pierogi or gnocchi should melt in the mouth. They are also a great vehicle for a variety of sauces, which can create a meal. Mixed with the veal and morel sauce, for example, they will satisfy big appetites.

I make a distinction between two types of dumplings—gnocchi and pierogi. In the former, the dumpling consists of mashed potatoes, flour, and sometimes eggs; in the latter, the dumpling is a ravioli stuffed with mashed potatoes.

I use all-purpose potatoes for the gnocchi-type dumplings. They have less starch and the dumplings are light. I use baking potatoes for the stuffing in the pierogi-type dumplings because they make the best mashed potatoes.

Dumplings are poached in boiling water or broth, drained and sauced. The dumplings generally can be prepared ahead of time, but I do not advise freezing them as it diminishes the flavor and transforms them into bullets.

German Potato Dumplings with a Veal and Morel Sauce

This dish is the creation of a quintessential home cook, Inge Wilkinson, who cooks by instinct and never remembers how to cook the same dish twice. I came prepared with my measuring cups and paper and pencil when she cooked this succulent dish. I had morels in the house when Inge cooked, but the sauce is equally good made with dry Boletus edulis *(cep in English, cèpes in French, porcini in Italian, or Polish mushrooms). Because of the work involved, I make this dish for a crowd, but the recipe can be cut in half easily. (You may prepare the sauce ahead of time; it improves with reheating.)*

VEAL AND MOREL SAUCE:

1 1/4 ounces (2/3 cup) dried morels or ceps
2 tablespoons butter or margarine
3 tablespoons olive oil
3 pounds boned veal breast, cut into 1-inch cubes, fat removed
Flour for dredging
2 cups peeled and chopped onions
6 garlic cloves, peeled and chopped
2 cups white wine (Chardonnay)
4 Italian canned tomatoes, drained, or 2 large fresh tomatoes, chopped
1 strip lemon peel
1 teaspoon salt
Lots of freshly ground black pepper
1/2 cup heavy cream
Chopped fresh parsley

THE POTATOES:

2 pounds all-purpose potatoes such as Yukon Gold, White Rose, or Superior
2 teaspoons salt
2 eggs
About 1 1/2 cups flour
2 tablespoons unsalted butter, melted

Place the morels or ceps (porcini) in a colander and scrub under cold water to remove sand. Soak them in 2 cups warm water for 1 hour (2 hours for ceps).

Heat 1 tablespoon butter and 2 tablespoons oil in a large skillet. Dredge the veal in flour, shaking off the excess. Brown the veal in the skillet in several batches, stirring occasionally. Transfer the meat to a dutch oven.

Heat the remaining 1 tablespoon oil in the skillet and sauté the chopped onions and garlic for 1 minute. Be careful not to burn them. Add to the veal.

Strain the morel liquid through a strainer lined with paper towels and press the water out of the morels.

Deglaze the skillet with the morel liquid and white wine. Bring to a boil and boil for 2 minutes. Pour over the veal. Add the tomatoes and the strip of lemon peel. Season with salt and freshly ground black pepper. Cover and simmer over low heat for 1½ to 2 hours, or until the meat is tender.

With a slotted spoon, remove the meat and reserve. Strain the sauce, pushing down on the tomatoes, onion, and garlic to extract all the juices. Pour the strained juices back over the meat.

In a small skillet, melt the remaining 1 tablespoon butter and briefly sauté the reserved morels (about 1 minute). Add the cream and fresh parsley. Stir and pour over the meat. Reheat when ready to spoon over the dumplings.

In a large saucepan, cover the potatoes with cold salted water and bring to a boil. Partially cover and cook for 30 minutes, or until tender.

Drain and peel the potatoes. Mash them with a potato masher, a ricer, or through a strainer, 1 potato at a time.

In a large bowl, combine the mashed potatoes with the salt, eggs, and a little more than 1 cup of flour. Start kneading with your hands to smooth out the mixture. After several minutes of kneading, add a bit more flour if the dough becomes too sticky. Knead until the dough is smooth.

Dust a work surface with flour. Cut the dough into 5 pieces. Dust flour on your hands and start rolling each piece of dough into a thin sausage about 2 feet long. Cut each sausage into 1-inch-long dumplings, and flatten each lightly with the back of a fork.

Preheat the oven to 300 degrees and butter a 3-quart baking dish.

In a large amount of simmering salted water, poach the dumplings in 3 batches. When they reach the surface of the water,

(continued)

count 2 minutes and then drain them in a colander. Put the dumplings in the prepared baking dish, dribbling melted butter over them and tossing to prevent them from sticking to each other.

Ladle the sauce and the meat over the dumplings and bake for 10 to 15 minutes.

NOTE: The dumplings can be poached and combined with the sauce several hours before serving. Bake at the last minute.

Serves 8

Italian Gnocchi

1½ pounds all-purpose potatoes such as Yukon Gold, White Rose, or Superior

About 1 cup flour

1½ teaspoons salt

In a large saucepan, cover the potatoes with cold salted water. Bring to a boil, partially cover, and cook for 30 minutes, or until tender.

Drain and peel as soon as you can handle the potatoes. Mash them with a potato masher, ricer, or through a strainer, 1 potato at a time.

In a large bowl, combine the mashed potatoes with 1½ teaspoons salt and 1 cup of flour. After several minutes of kneading with your hands, add more flour if the dough is too sticky. Knead until the dough is soft and smooth.

Dust a work surface with flour. Cut the dough into four pieces, dust your hands with flour and roll each piece of dough into a long thin sausage, about ½ inch thick. Cut each sausage into 1-inch-long gnocchi.

Place a gnocchi in the concave part of the fork and with your floured index finger make an indentation in the center. Flip the gnocchi onto a floured cookie sheet.

Preheat the oven to 300 degrees and heat an oiled 3-quart baking dish.

In a large pot of simmering salted water, poach the gnocchi in 2 batches. When they reach the surface of the water, count 2 minutes. With a slotted spoon transfer the gnocchi into the preheated baking dish. Dribble 1 tablespoon olive oil over them and shake the pan to prevent them from sticking to each other.

Pour the sauce of your choice over the gnocchi and bake for 10 minutes in the preheated oven.

Serves 6

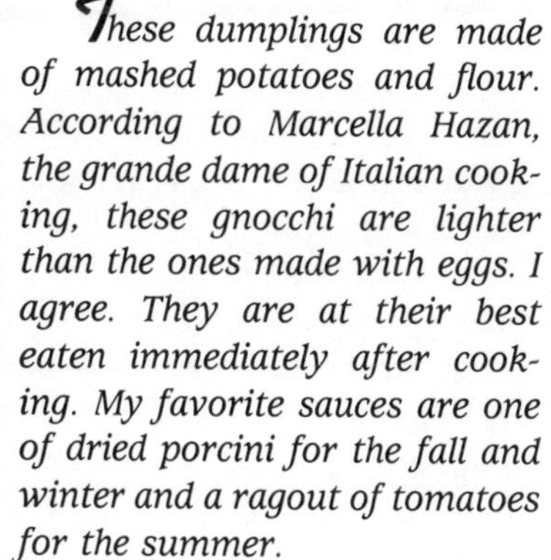

These dumplings are made of mashed potatoes and flour. According to Marcella Hazan, the grande dame of Italian cooking, these gnocchi are lighter than the ones made with eggs. I agree. They are at their best eaten immediately after cooking. My favorite sauces are one of dried porcini for the fall and winter and a ragout of tomatoes for the summer.

Porcini Sauce

This sauce is good on mashed potatoes, gnocchi, pasta, and rice. Boletus edulis, *the Latin name for ceps (porcini), has an interesting history. Because of their strong nutty taste, porcini dishes concealed poison when the Romans needed to get rid of someone. But on the brighter side, the porcini was believed to remove freckles and blemishes, and Bohemian lumberjacks believe they prevent cancer. In the States, the cep, as it is called in English, is easily found in its dried form all year long in supermarkets under the Italian name porcini or under the French name cèpes. I priced it in several stores and found the mushroom is cheaper to buy under its Italian name than under its French one!*

1 1/2 cups (3 ounces) dried porcini
2 tablespoons olive oil
1 teaspoon salt
1/2 cup heavy cream
1 tablespoon minced fresh tarragon, or 1 teaspoon dried tarragon
6 tablespoons (3/4 stick) unsalted butter or margarine

Put the mushrooms in a strainer and scrub them under cold water to remove sand. Soak the porcini in 3 cups warm water for 2 hours. Strain through cheesecloth, reserving the mushrooms and their liquid.

Heat the olive oil in a large skillet, add the porcini, and stir-fry for 1 minute. Add salt, cover, and braise for 5 minutes over medium heat.

Uncover, turn the heat up, and pour in 1/2 cup of the porcini liquid. Reduce it by half. Repeat this procedure until there is 1 cup of liquid left to boil down. Pour in the last cup of porcini liquid, the cream, tarragon, and butter, cut up in pieces. Boil down until the sauce gets slightly syrupy. Taste and correct seasoning. Reheat the sauce before combining with gnocchi, or other starch of your choice.

Makes 2 cups

Ragout of Fresh Tomatoes and Bacon or Pancetta

3 pounds tomatoes
2 tablespoons olive oil
4 ounces slab bacon or pancetta, diced into 1/4-inch cubes (1 cup)
3 garlic cloves, peeled and finely chopped
1 1/2 teaspoons salt
1 teaspoon sugar
2 sprigs fresh thyme
1 cup grated Gruyère or 1/4 cup grated Parmesan

When tomatoes are really tomatoes, in the middle of the summer, I make this sauce. It's summer in one dish, great over pasta as well as gnocchi.

Bring several quarts of water to a boil. Plunge in the tomatoes for 30 seconds and transfer them to a large bowl of cold water. Peel and squeeze the tomatoes to extrude liquid and seeds. Chop flesh coarsely.

Heat the oil in a large skillet and sauté the bacon or pancetta. As soon as it browns, add the chopped tomatoes, garlic, salt, and sugar. Stir and, finally, bury the sprigs of fresh thyme in the tomatoes. Cook over medium heat for 15 minutes, stirring once in a while. This sauce will keep at this point for several days in the refrigerator.

Reheat the sauce, fold in the Gruyère or Parmesan. Taste and correct seasoning.

To use with gnocchi, pour the sauce over and bake in a 300-degree oven for 10 minutes.

Makes about 3 cups

I made up this sauce especially for canned tomatoes to serve during the tomatoless months.

Winter Tomato Sauce with Goat Cheese

Two 28-ounce cans Italian plum tomatoes, drained and chopped (save the juice)
1/4 cup olive oil
1/2 cup peeled chopped shallots
4 garlic cloves, peeled and minced
Half a hot jalapeño pepper, minced (seeds included)
1 cup red wine
1 teaspoon salt
1 teaspoon sugar
2 teaspoons dried thyme or oregano
8 ounces Bucheron goat cheese

Boil the tomato liquid to half its original volume and set aside.

In a large skillet, heat the olive oil. Add the shallots, garlic, and the jalapeño pepper and seeds. Cover and braise over low heat for 10 minutes.

Add the tomatoes, tomato liquid, red wine, salt, sugar, and thyme or oregano to the shallot mixture. Stir, cover, and simmer over low heat for 40 minutes.

Discard the rind of the cheese. Crumble the cheese over the tomato sauce. Cover and cook for an additional 5 minutes, or until the cheese is melted. Correct seasoning.

Makes 4 cups

French Gnocchi with Mornay Sauce

2 pounds all-purpose potatoes such as Yukon Gold, White Rose, or Superior
2 teaspoons salt
Freshly ground black pepper
Pâte à Choux (page 11)
2 tablespoons melted butter
Mornay Sauce (recipe follows)

In a saucepan, cover the potatoes with cold salted water. Bring to a boil, partially cover, and cook for 30 minutes, or until tender.

Drain the potatoes and reserve ⅔ cup potato water. Peel and mash the potatoes with a masher, ricer, or through a strainer, 1 potato at a time.

Mix the potato water and the mashed potatoes. Season with salt and freshly ground pepper. Combine the mashed potatoes with the pâte à choux.

Preheat the oven to 300 degrees; butter a 3-quart baking dish.

Dust flour on a work surface and cut the dough into 4 pieces. Dust hands with flour and roll out each piece of dough into a 24-inch-long sausage. Cut each sausage into 1-inch gnocchi and keep on towels dusted with flour.

Poach the gnocchi in 4 batches in a large amount of salted water. When the gnocchi reach the surface of the water, count 1 minute, remove, and drain in a colander.

Put the gnocchi in the prepared baking dish, dribble the melted butter over them, and toss to prevent them from sticking to each other.

Ladle mornay sauce over the gnocchi and bake in the oven for 10 minutes. Turn on the broiler and gratiné the top for 1 minute, or until it is golden brown.

Serves 8

A béchamel (a white sauce) with cheese, sauce mornay is a favorite among French children. French mothers disguise vegetables with a mornay sauce. Poured over gnocchi, it's a meal.

MORNAY SAUCE

3 tablespoons butter
3 tablespoons flour
3 cups boiling milk
1 onion, peeled and chopped
1 teaspoon salt
Freshly ground pepper
1 cup grated Gruyère or
  1/4 cup grated Parmesan

Melt the butter in a heavy saucepan. Whisk in the flour. Cook 1 minute, whisking constantly over medium heat. Pour in half the boiling milk. Whisk until smooth and add the remaining boiling milk. Add the onion, salt, and pepper and cook for 20 minutes over low heat, whisking once in a while to prevent a skin from forming on top. Add more milk if the sauce gets too thick. (It should have the consistency of buttermilk.) Fold in the cheese.

Pierogi-Ziemniaki

PIEROGI WITH POTATO AND FARMER'S CHEESE STUFFING

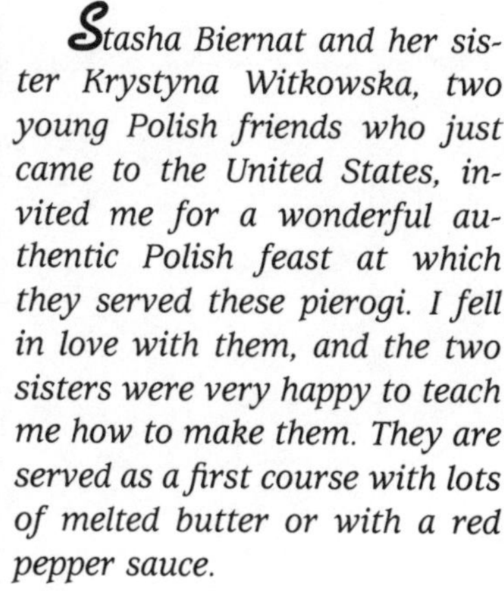

Stasha Biernat and her sister Krystyna Witkowska, two young Polish friends who just came to the United States, invited me for a wonderful authentic Polish feast at which they served these pierogi. I fell in love with them, and the two sisters were very happy to teach me how to make them. They are served as a first course with lots of melted butter or with a red pepper sauce.

1 pound russet potatoes, peeled and quartered (3 cups)
3 tablespoons olive oil
1 medium onion, peeled and minced
8 ounces farmer's cheese
2 teaspoons salt
½ teaspoon freshly ground pepper
2½ cups unbleached flour
½ beaten egg
10 tablespoons (1¼ sticks) unsalted butter, or Red Pepper Sauce (recipe follows)

In a saucepan, cover the potatoes with cold salted water. Bring to a boil, partially cover, and cook for 20 minutes, or until tender.

Meanwhile, heat the olive oil in a skillet over moderate heat. Add the onion and cook, stirring occasionally, until soft but not browned, about 5 minutes. Drain the potatoes and mash them with a potato masher or through a ricer or strainer, 1 potato at a time.

Thoroughly combine the potatoes, onion, cheese, 1½ teaspoons salt, and freshly ground pepper. Taste and correct seasoning.

The hand method for the pierogi: In a medium bowl, combine the flour, ¾ cup warm water, beaten egg, and ½ teaspoon salt. Turn out onto a floured surface and knead the dough, adding more flour if necessary, until smooth, about 7 minutes.

The food processor method: Combine the beaten egg and warm water in a small bowl. Place the flour and salt in the food processor bowl and process for 5 seconds. With the machine on, pour in the water and egg mixture. Process for 20 seconds. The dough will still be slightly sticky to the touch; do not overprocess. If the dough sticks to your fingers and breaks off easily, add 2 tablespoons additional flour and process for 10 seconds.

(continued)

The hand method to roll out the dough: Cut the dough into 4 pieces. Cover and let rest for 1 hour. Flour the pastry surface and rolling pin and start rolling each piece as thin as possible into a 10-inch circle.

The pasta machine method: Cut the dough into 4 batches. Flatten each batch with the palm of your hand and roll in a pasta machine, starting with the thick setting and progressing to the next-to-thinnest setting.

Using a round 3-inch cutter, stamp out circles of dough. Gather the scraps together. Repeat with the remaining batches of dough. Roll out the scraps and cut into more circles.

Fill each circle with 1 teaspoon potato filling. Brush cold water around the edges. Fold each circle into a half-moon, and press with your fingertips to close the edges. Press with the tines of a fork to seal. Keep the pierogi on a towel dusted with flour.

Poach the pierogi in 2 batches in a large amount of boiling salted water. When they reach the surface, count 2 minutes and remove to a bowl of warm water. Drain and transfer to a heated serving dish. Keep warm in a low oven.

Meanwhile, in a small skillet, heat the butter over moderate heat until it starts to brown. Drizzle the hot butter over the pierogi, or serve them with the red pepper sauce.

Makes about 60 pierogi, serving 12 for a first course

RED PEPPER SAUCE

FOR THE GARNISH:

1 red bell pepper
1 yellow pepper

FOR THE SAUCE:

2 pounds red bell peppers
¼ cup olive oil
1 cup Light Potato Soup (page 24) or 1 cup chicken broth
1¼ teaspoons salt
⅛ teaspoon cayenne
1 cup heavy cream
Freshly ground pepper

For the garnish: Quarter the red and yellow peppers. Discard the core and seeds. Cut each quarter into three strips. Shave off the inside meat of the peppers, leaving the outer skin with just a fine layer of flesh. (Cook the shavings with the peppers below.) Slice into very thin strips. Set aside.

For the sauce: Slice off the stem ends of the peppers; discard the seeds and center core. Cut the peppers in long strips first, then cut them crosswise into 1-inch cubes.

In a 6-quart dutch oven, heat 3 tablespoons olive oil; add the pepper cubes and stir. Add the stock and season with 1 teaspoon salt and cayenne. Cover and simmer over low to medium heat for 1 hour, or until the peppers are soft.

Process the peppers and juices for 2 minutes in a food processor. Strain the sauce to discard the skins, pushing it with the back of a spoon through a strainer.

Reheat the sauce, adding the cream. Taste and correct seasoning.

For the garnish: Heat the remaining 1 tablespoon olive oil in a nonstick skillet and sauté the peppers for the garnish for 1 minute. Season with the remaining ¼ teaspoon salt and freshly ground pepper.

(continued)

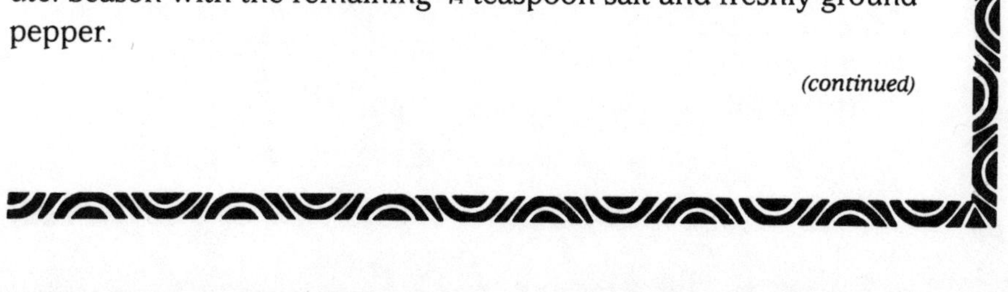

For the presentation: Ladle the sauce in the center of individual warm plates, decorate with the pierogi, and sprinkle several strips of peppers on top.

Makes about 2¼ cups

Les Crozets aux Pommes de Terre et Fromages

FRENCH DUMPLINGS STUFFED WITH POTATOES AND CHEESES

These dumplings, the French answer to Polish pierogi, are called crozets *in the southern part of the Dauphine Province, which neighbors Provence on the south and Italy on the east. I learned to make* crozets *from Juliette Rasclard, a neighbor. She stuffs them with mashed potatoes and homemade Picodon, a goat cheese special to the Drome region. Near the Italian frontier, in Briançon, mozzarella replaces picodon. I use both of them, substituting Bucheron for picodon in the States.*

1 pound russet potatoes, peeled and quartered (3 cups)
Salt and pepper
5 tablespoons olive oil
¼ cup shredded fresh basil (in season) or ¼ cup minced fresh curly parsley
⅔ pound mozzarella, grated (2¼ cups)
⅓ pound goat cheese (Bucheron), grated (1½ cups)
2 large garlic cloves, peeled and minced
8 cups chicken or turkey broth, or Light Potato Soup (page 24)
Fresh Noodle Dough (recipe follows)
1 cup grated Parmesan or Gruyère

In a saucepan, cover the potatoes with salted cold water. Bring the water to a boil, partially cover, and cook for 20 minutes, or until the potatoes are tender.

Drain and mash the potatoes with a potato masher, a ricer, or through a strainer. Add salt, pepper, and 2 tablespoons of the olive oil. Set aside.

Stack the basil leaves, roll them like a cigarette and slice into very thin shreds. Set aside. Mix the cheeses and garlic with the remaining 3 tablespoons olive oil. Season with salt and pepper. Mix in the mashed potatoes.

Prepare the noodle dough. Stamp 3-inch circles out of the dough. Gather the scraps together and cover them. Repeat with the remaining batches of dough. Roll out the scraps and cut into circles. Fill each circle with 1 teaspoon stuffing. Brush cold water on the edge and fold over into a half-moon, sealing the dumplings by pushing down all around the rim with the back of a fork.

Place on a cookie sheet dusted with cornmeal. They will keep, refrigerated, for several hours before poaching.

When ready to eat, heat 2 large skillets with 4 cups of rich stock in each and add the shredded basil or chopped parsley.

Shake the cornmeal from the dumplings. Poach in the stock for 3 or 4 minutes.

Place 3 or 4 dumplings in each of the 8 soup plates and ladle 1 cup of stock over them. Serve the Parmesan at the table.

Makes about 30 dumplings, serving 8

FRESH NOODLE DOUGH

2 cups all-purpose flour
2 eggs
1/3 cup cream
1/2 teaspoon salt

The food processor method: In the bowl of the food processor fitted with the steel blade, combine the flour, eggs, cream, and salt. Process until a ball is made, about 20 seconds. If the dough is very sticky, knead in more flour.

By hand: Place the flour on a work surface and make a 10-inch well in the center. Add the eggs, cream, and salt. With the back of a fork, beat the eggs and cream together. Gradually incorporate the flour, starting from the inside rim of the well. When all the flour is incorporated, knead into a smooth dough, adding more flour if the dough is sticky.

Cut the dough into 4 pieces. Roll each piece into a 10-inch circle or put through a pasta machine, starting with the widest setting. Dust the dough with flour between each setting if it is too sticky. Roll out at the next to the last setting. Roll twice through that setting. You should have a strip that is about 2 1/2 feet long. Dust the counter with cornmeal. Put the strip on the counter, cover with plastic, and continue with the next 3 pieces.

French Dumplings Stuffed with Potatoes, Romaine, and Garlic

- 1 head of romaine
- 1/4 teaspoon salt
- 3 tablespoons drippings from a roast, or 3 tablespoons olive oil
- 3 garlic cloves, peeled and minced
- 1/2 cup minced parsley

Remove the center stems of the romaine and discard. Wash the romaine under cold running water. Place the wet leaves in a large skillet. Add the salt, cover, and braise until the romaine is soft. Mince fine; you should have 2 cups.

Heat the drippings or olive oil, add the minced garlic, and sauté, stirring constantly over high heat, for 1 minute. Add the romaine and parsley. Cook for 5 minutes, stirring occasionally. Combine this stuffing with mashed potatoes, following the preceding recipe, and proceed to make and poach the dumplings.

This is another favorite stuffing of my friends in the Drôme. It is a mixture of cooked greens, highly seasoned with minced garlic and leftover drippings from a roast. Meats are braised more than roasted in the Drôme, which makes for wonderful drippings used in gratins or in stuffings. Substitute olive oil if necessary.

11. Potato Pancakes

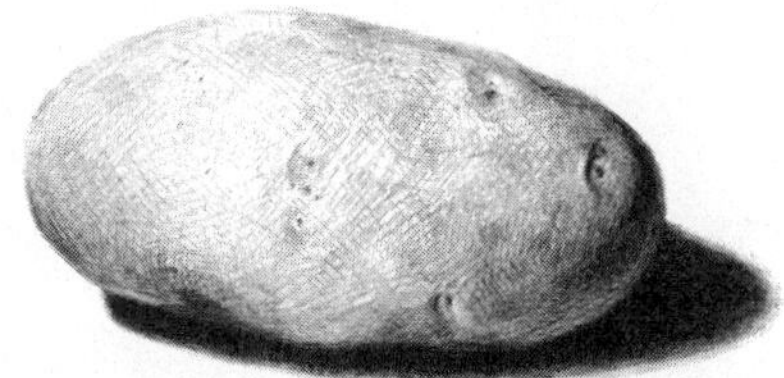

Potato pancakes are made with all kinds of all-purpose, waxy, or baking potatoes: red potatoes, (large Nordland or Pontiac), California White Rose, Yukon Gold, Maine Superior or Long Island Kennebec, Katahdin, and the russet. For pancakes, the raw potatoes are grated or sliced, or they are boiled first and then grated or sliced.

When the potatoes are grated raw, they can be mixed with flour and eggs to make a loose pancake batter, or with herbs, garlic, or shallots without flour and eggs. When the potatoes are boiled first, they are mashed or grated, shaped into a pancake, and fried; or the potatoes are sliced and fried or baked in the oven.

There are different gadgets on the market to grate potatoes, from a simple tool like the kitchen hand grater or a mouli-julienne, to a professional mandoline and the grater blade of a food processor. Depending on the texture wanted, the potatoes are grated from coarse to nearly a purée. For latkes, I grate the potatoes on the coarse side of a hand grater or with the coarse blade of the food processor; on the other hand, for boxty, I switch to the fine side of the hand grater (I wear oven mittens when I do this) for a very fine texture.

For the *crique*, a potato pancake that has no flour and no eggs, I plunge the raw grated potatoes in cold water to wash out the starch; otherwise the pancake will be gummy. For the potato pancakes made with a batter of eggs and flour, I do not wash off the starch, I just drain the grated potatoes in a kitchen strainer, lightly pushing on the potatoes with the back of a spoon to squeeze moisture out of them.

Potato pancakes are made all over the world; made with raw potatoes, they are called latkes in Yiddish, frittata in Italian, tortilla in Spanish, *criques* in French. Made with twice-cooked potatoes, the pancakes are the American hash browns, the Swiss roesti or *reuchsti*, the French *macaire*. The Irish boxty stands alone: it's made with raw and twice-cooked potatoes.

La Crique Ardèchoise

The Ardèche region is west of the Rhône River in southern France. In this region, potato pancakes are called criques, *and must be flipped 7 times—that's the local rule. A* crique *is a thin crunchy pancake of grated potatoes with a mixture of parsley and garlic, sautéed in oil. The amount of garlic is up to the cook. The Ardèchoise flips her* criques *in the air like a crêpe. It is at first intimidating to flip them, but it gets easier once a crust forms on both sides. The first time I made a* crique, *I was*

2 pounds Yukon Gold, large Red Pontiac, Nordland, Superior, or russet potatoes, peeled and coarsely grated
2 tablespoons peeled minced garlic
¼ cup minced parsley
1 teaspoon salt
Freshly ground pepper
¼ cup corn oil

Cover the grated potatoes with cold water to wash off the surface starch. (If this step is eliminated, the pancake will taste gummy.) Drain and push on the potatoes with the back of a cake turner, extracting as much water as possible.

In a bowl, combine the potatoes, garlic, parsley, salt, and freshly ground pepper. Divide the mixture into 2 batches.

Heat 2 tablespoons oil in each of two 10-inch nonstick skillets. When the oil is very hot, spread half the potato mixture in each pan, packing down with a cake turner, forming a neat pancake. Cook 8 to 10 minutes over medium heat, occasionally pushing down on the pancake and shaking the pan to loosen it.

Put a large plate on top of each skillet, drain the oil, and invert the *criques* onto the plate. The tops should be crusty. With care, slide them back into their skillets with the oil (it's a little tricky at first because the underside of the pancake is raw). Cook the pancakes for 8 minutes more, occasionally pushing down on them with the back of a pancake turner to extract moisture and shaking the pan to keep the pancake loose in the skillet.

Now, invert the *criques* every 3 or 4 minutes 5 more times. If you feel brave, start flipping them in the air, but not before both sides of the pancakes are crusty. (I generally start doing it after the third inversion.) Try it, it's fun.

Cut the *criques* in wedges with a pair of scissors (easier than cutting with a knife).

Serves 4 for dinner, 8 as an appetizer

emboldened by my success and could not stop flipping, forgetting the 7-flip rule.

In the Ardèche, the criques *are served for supper with a tossed green salad, or sometimes for an afternoon break, when farmers' wives take them to their husbands working in the fields. These are great for an appetizer, too.*

Latkes

These latkes are an adaptation of the latke recipe in Raymond Sokolov and Susan Friedland's book: The Jewish-American Kitchen. *They are superb. If you serve them as a main dish, try them with a tossed green salad and cold roasted chicken.*

1 1/2 pounds russet potatoes
1 large onion, peeled
2 large eggs
2 tablespoons all-purpose flour
2 teaspoons salt
Freshly ground black pepper
About 1/2 cup peanut oil, light olive oil, or rendered chicken fat

Peel and grate the potatoes using the largest holes on a 4-sided grater. If you prefer to use a processor, fit it with the grater with the largest holes and shred.

Grate the onion in the same manner.

Transfer the grated potatoes and onion to a kitchen strainer placed over a large bowl. Press out the excess moisture with a wooden spoon and transfer the vegetables to another bowl.

Pour off all the liquid from the first bowl, leaving behind the potato starch that settles at the bottom.

Break the eggs into the bowl with the potato starch and beat together. Mix in the potato-onion mixture and add the flour. Season with salt and freshly ground pepper. Now it's a matter of preference. You can cook the latkes right away and you will have latkes that are very crispy all the way through, or you can wait 1 hour before making them. The batter will thin out while waiting, and the potatoes and the onion will render more liquid. The cooked latkes will then be crisp outside and moist inside. It's up to you.

Spread several layers of paper towels flat on the counter. Heat 1/3 cup oil or rendered chicken fat in a large nonstick skillet. When the fat is hot, quickly drop in about 3 tablespoons of potato-onion mixture and flatten it out to a 3 1/2-inch disk; repeat twice. (You should be able to make 3 latkes at a time.) Peek after 1 minute, and when the underside is golden brown, turn the latkes over and fry the other side until golden brown.

Remove the latkes with a skimmer, draining the fat back into the skillet, and place them on paper towels. Transfer them to a preheated platter and keep warm in a 200-degree oven while you fry the rest.

Serve with sour cream, yogurt, or applesauce.

Makes 18 3-½-inch latkes, serving 6 for an appetizer, 4 for a main dish

Czechoslovakian Potato Pancakes

- 2 pounds unpeeled russet potatoes, coarsely grated
- 3 tablespoons flour
- 1 onion, peeled and grated
- 3 eggs, beaten
- 1½ teaspoons salt
- 1 teaspoon sugar

Combine all ingredients and beat well. Follow the instructions in the preceding recipe to cook the pancakes.

Makes 18 4-inch pancakes, serving 6

These are Mrs. Jarson's potato pancakes. Her daughter, my friend Elizabeth Hamer, remembers that ". . . we always ate the pancakes folded around sour cream. I remember my mother and father working in the kitchen together, and we three kids would eat them as fast as they could make them . . ."

Pachade

GRATED POTATO PANCAKE, AUVERGNAT STYLE

The Auvergne, a mountainous region in the center of France, is known to have a strong Jewish community. Latkes seem to have influenced the pachade, *though the Auvergnats include bacon.*

1 pound Yukon Gold, Red Pontiac, Nordland, Superior, or russet potatoes, peeled and coarsely grated
2½ ounces lean bacon, diced
1 teaspoon oil
2 beaten eggs
1 teaspoon salt
Freshly ground pepper

Drain the grated potatoes in a strainer, lightly pushing on them with the back of a spoon. You should have about 1½ cups.

In a 10-inch nonstick skillet, cook the bacon with the oil until barely crisp.

Combine the grated potatoes with the eggs and season with salt and freshly ground pepper.

Pour the potato mixture into the skillet over the bacon and press down on the mixture to flatten it. Cook uncovered over medium heat for 8 to 10 minutes. Shake the pan occasionally to loosen the pancake.

When the bottom of the *pachade* is golden brown, drain off the fat and invert on a plate. Pour the fat back into the skillet and slide the pancake back in. Cook for 5 minutes or until the bottom is brown.

Serves 2

Pachade with Morels

¾ ounce (⅓ cup) dried morels

2 tablespoons unsalted butter or margarine

Soak the morels in ½ cup warm water for ½ hour. Strain through cheesecloth, reserving the liquid. Wash the morels under cold water to be sure to remove any dirt or grit. If they are small, leave them whole; coarsely chop large ones.

Heat 2 tablespoons butter or margarine in a 10-inch nonstick skillet and sauté the morels for 1 minute. Pour in half the reserved liquid and boil down; add the remaining liquid and boil down until the liquid has evaporated.

Follow the instructions in the preceding recipe to make the pancake.

Here, you substitute morels for bacon.

BOXTY

**Boxty-on-the-griddle, boxty-in-the-pan,
If you don't eat boxty, you'll never get your man.**

That's what happens to Irish girls who do not eat boxty. In *Feasting Galore—Recipes and Food Lore from Ireland*, by Maura Laverty, the author tells of the warning: "In the north and west of Ireland, boxty sometimes takes the place of the Halloween barmbrack as a prognosticator of the year's weddings. A ring wrapped in wax paper is mixed in with the batter. Whoever gets it will marry within the year." In the east and south, the ring is buried in colcannon, mashed potatoes with kale.

Boxty on the Griddle

1 cup mashed potatoes
About 3/4 cup finely grated raw potatoes (14 ounces Yukon Gold or Superior potatoes)
1 scant cup all-purpose flour
About 3 tablespoons bacon fat
1 1/2 teaspoons salt
Freshly ground pepper
Butter

If you don't have leftover mashed potatoes, cover 1/2 pound potatoes with cold salted water. Partially cover and cook for 20 minutes, or until tender. Drain, peel, and mash the potatoes with an old-fashioned potato masher, ricer, or through a strainer. Measure 1 cup of mashed potato and set aside.

Drain the grated potatoes in a strainer, pushing down with the back of a spoon. Reserve the potato water, as it might be necessary later on.

Combine the raw grated potatoes and the mashed potatoes with a fork. Gradually beat in the flour, tablespoon by tablespoon, 2 tablespoons bacon fat, and the salt and pepper; knead until smooth. If the dough gets too dry, add some reserved potato water.

Cut the dough into 4 pieces. Flour a pastry surface and shape each piece into a pancake 5 inches round. Cut an X on the top.

Heat the remaining bacon fat in a large nonstick skillet. Add the boxties and cook for 15 minutes on each side, or until golden brown.

Slice the boxties into wedges, spreading butter over each wedge. Serve immediately. The butter melting into the boxty is a real treat.

Serves 4 to 6

My friend Bernadette O'Brien's grandmother served boxty dipped in hot milk at tea time when the children came home from school. They ate it hot from the skillet, cut into individual wedges. Each wedge is cut sandwichlike, with butter spread inside the sandwich. It's also wonderful dipped in hot tea.

For breakfast, try leftover boxty. Cut it into thin slices and fry it in sizzling butter or margarine. Serve with jam or maple syrup.

Boxty in the Pan

¾ pound small russet potatoes, peeled
1½ cups sifted flour
4 teaspoons baking powder
1 teaspoon salt
3 beaten eggs
1 cup milk
4 tablespoons (½ stick) butter, melted
1 tablespoon bacon fat
Butter for serving

Finely grate 1 potato and drain in a strainer, lightly pushing on it with the back of a spoon. You should have about ¼ cup grated potato.

Cut the remaining potatoes into 1-inch cubes. In a saucepan, cover them with cold salted water and bring to a boil. Partially cover and cook for 10 to 15 minutes, or until the potatoes are tender. Drain and mash the potatoes. You should have ¾ cup firmly packed mashed potatoes.

On wax paper, sift together flour, baking powder, and salt; set aside.

Combine the eggs, milk, and melted butter.

In a large mixing bowl, mix the grated potato with the mashed potato. With a large fork, stir in the flour mixture and the egg mixture.

Preheat the oven to 425 degrees.

Spoon bacon fat into a 9-inch cast-iron skillet. Place it in the oven for 3 minutes to heat the fat and the pan. Remove the pan from the oven and swirl the bacon fat over the bottom. Add the batter.

Return pan to the oven and bake until the top is golden brown—35 to 40 minutes. The boxty puffs up like a soufflé. Loosely cover it if the top browns too fast.

Cut into wedges and serve hot, right from the pan, with extra butter, the traditional way.

For dinner, I serve the boxty with a mixture of yogurt, basil, and garlic.

Serves 4 to 6

YOGURT, BASIL, AND GARLIC SAUCE

1 cup plain yogurt
Handful fresh basil leaves
3 garlic cloves, peeled and coarsely chopped
Salt
Pepper

In the bowl of the food processor, combine yogurt, basil, and garlic. Process until smooth. Season with salt and pepper.

TWICE-COOKED POTATO PANCAKES

The day before or several hours before making a twice-cooked potato pancake, cover the unpeeled potatoes with cold salted water. Bring to a boil, partially cover, and cook for 30 to 35 minutes, or until tender when pierced with a knife. Quickly drain the potatoes. Set aside until cold. Peel the potatoes when you are ready to cook.

Here I offer a sampling of twice-cooked potatoes from around the world; from the States hash browns, from France potato *macaire*, and from Ecuador *llapingachos*.

Hash Browns

There are many versions of hash browns but as my sister-in-law, Marilyn Dabner, says, there is no exact recipe for hash browns, you just do it with left-over boiled potatoes. Fry the potatoes in butter, margarine, or oil, shaped into small or large, thick or thin pancakes.

Wait until the fat is hot before cooking the pancakes; otherwise the outside crust will not be crunchy enough and it will be difficult to invert the pancakes.

Two 10-inch nonstick skillets

3 pounds russet potatoes, boiled, peeled cold, and coarsely grated (6 cups)
1½ teaspoons salt
Freshly ground pepper
½ cup corn oil

Season the grated potatoes with salt and freshly ground pepper.

Heat 2 tablespoons oil in each of two 10-inch nonstick skillets. When hot, add 3 cups of grated potatoes to each skillet. Form a flat cake by gently pressing down with a pancake turner on each batch.

Cook 5 to 6 minutes over high heat, until the bottom of the pancakes forms a crust. Run a spatula around the edges to keep the cake loose and shake the pan gently from time to time.

Place a plate over each skillet, and invert the pancakes. Add 2 more tablespoons oil to each skillet. When the fat is very hot, slide them back into the skillets and cook for another 5 or 6 minutes. Slide them on to a platter and serve immediately.

Serves 6

Potato Macaire

1 1/2 pounds Yukon Gold, large Red Pontiac, Nordland, Superior, or russet potatoes, boiled, peeled cold, and sliced 1/8 inch thick (4 cups)
Salt
1 teaspoon freshly ground pepper
4 tablespoons (1/2 stick) unsalted butter or margarine, cut into shavings

Preheat the oven to 375 degrees. Butter a 10-inch square ovenproof baking dish.

Overlap half of the potatoes in 1 layer in the baking dish and season with salt and freshly ground pepper. Dot the top with 2 tablespoons butter or margarine. Layer the remaining potato slices and dot with butter or margarine. Season with salt and freshly ground pepper. Cover the potatoes with foil and bake in the center of the oven for 45 minutes.

Set the broiler on high; uncover the potatoes and put under the broiler for 1 minute, just to color the top. Serve immediately, right from the pan.

Serves 4

Anna of the mashed potatoes (see page 106) advises us to peel and slice cooked potatoes cold; the potatoes will not absorb too much butter or margarine. The fat gives a wonderful flavor (especially if you are able to use butter) but does not penetrate the potatoes.

Llapingachos

ECUADORIAN POTATO CAKES

The Ecuadorians serve llapingachos, *pronounced "ya-pin-ga-chos" with a tossed salad of lettuce, avocado, and tomatoes or topped with fried eggs for lunch and with fish for dinner.*

4 cups peeled and finely chopped onions
3 tablespoons butter or margarine
2 pounds russet potatoes, boiled, peeled cold, and finely grated (6 cups)
1 teaspoon salt
Freshly ground pepper
½ pound Muenster cheese, shredded (about 2 cups)
2 tablespoons olive oil

Braise the onions in the butter in a covered dutch oven for 20 minutes, or until soft but not browned. Set aside and cool.

Thoroughly mix the grated potatoes and onions. Season with 1 teaspoon salt and freshly ground pepper.

Shape the potato mixture into 12 balls about the size of golf balls. Make a deep well in each ball and bury about 3 tablespoons of cheese in each potato ball. Flatten each ball into a 3½-inch disk.

In a large skillet, heat 2 tablespoons olive oil and fry 4 *llapingachos* at a time for 3 or 4 minutes on each side. Add more oil if necessary.

Serves 6

Pancake l'Ami Louis

3 tablespoons goose fat
2 pounds unpeeled russet potatoes, sliced between 1/8 inch and 1/16 inch thick (6 cups)
1 1/2 teaspoons salt
Freshly ground pepper
1 tablespoon peeled minced garlic
1 tablespoon minced parsley

In a 10-inch nonstick skillet, melt the fat. Add the potato slices and stir-fry for 5 minutes. Sprinkle with salt and freshly ground pepper. Partially cover and cook over medium heat for 15 minutes.

Preheat the oven to 400 degrees.

Press down on the potatoes to shape them into a cake. Bake in the oven for 30 minutes. (Wrap the handle of your skillet with aluminum foil if it is not ovenproof.)

Invert on a serving dish, sprinkle with garlic and parsley, and serve immediately.

Serves 4

Many Americans visit the Paris restaurant Chez l'Ami Louis. *The menu there is short but good: foie gras or cèpes to start; a roast chicken or a leg of lamb served with fries or potato pancake for main courses. There is no dessert.*

The potatoes must be fried in goose fat to achieve the taste of l'Ami Louis's pancake. D'Artagnan, a company that specializes in fowl and foie gras, will mail-order foie gras and rendered goose fat (D'Artagnan, Inc., 339–419 St. Paul Avenue, Jersey City, N.J. 07306; tel. 1-800-DARTAGN). Goose fat can be kept for months in the freezer. Substitute chicken fat if necessary, but the dish will not be as tasty. At l'Ami Louis, the potatoes are peeled (the French would never think of leaving them unpeeled) but it's not really necessary.

Frittata Angela

Like many of my women friends, Angela is a natural cook who makes wonderful Italian dishes. Her cooking is very sensual as well as delicious; she caresses, talks to the food while preparing a meal. We made the frittata with all-purpose potatoes, but she frequently uses baking potatoes, too.

A frittata is good picnic food and looks very pretty on a buffet table.

1 1/2 pounds Yukon Gold or russet potatoes, peeled
1 large garlic clove, peeled
1 1/2 teaspoons salt
1 cup peeled minced onion
6 1/2 tablespoons olive oil
3 eggs
1 tablespoon milk
Freshly ground pepper
Italian parsley

With a sharp paring knife, slice the potatoes into small chips about the size of a quarter and about twice as thick, always turning the potato 1/8 of a turn each time you slice. You should have about 4 cups.

Wash the potatoes and pat dry. Mince the garlic clove with 1 teaspoon salt. With your hands, toss the potatoes, onion, and garlic with 1 tablespoon olive oil.

In a 10-inch nonstick skillet, heat 4 tablespoons oil and stir-fry the potato mixture for 5 minutes. Cover and braise until soft, about 20 minutes.

In a large bowl, beat the eggs with the milk, the remaining 1/2 teaspoon salt, and pepper. Fold in the cooked potato mixture.

Heat 1 1/2 tablespoons olive oil in the skillet, pour in the frittata, and cook for 10 minutes over medium heat, turning the pan 1/4 way every 5 minutes.

Invert the frittata on a plate and slide it back into the skillet for 3 minutes more. Turn onto a serving platter.

Decorate the top with several leaves of Italian parsley.

Serves 4

Tortilla

Follow the instructions for the frittata, adding 1 cup diced mixed green and red peppers to cook with the potatoes. Fry the frittata on one side only, and then invert on a serving dish. Decorate with thin rings of red and green peppers.

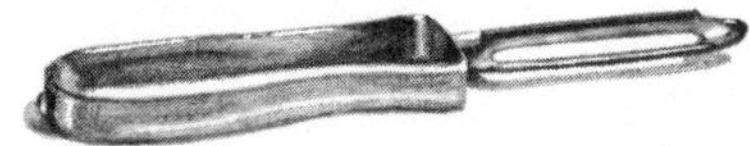

Wayne's Potato Omelet

2 tablespoons goose or chicken fat, or oil
2 cups cooked potatoes
6 eggs, beaten
Salt

In a skillet, heat 1 tablespoon fat and stir-fry the potatoes for 5 minutes. Set aside.

In a 7-inch nonstick skillet or omelet pan, melt 1 teaspoon fat. Swirl in 2 beaten eggs, salted, and stir the eggs for 10 seconds with a fork. Cook over medium high heat for 1 or 2 minutes or until the eggs are scrambled soft. Cover the eggs with 1/3 of the potatoes; with a fork, fold half the eggs over the potatoes. Cook 30 seconds more and invert the omelet onto a plate. Make 2 more omelets, adding a bit of fat if necessary, and serve immediately.

Serves 3

My husband does not mind cooking when I don't feel like it. He frisks the refrigerator for leftovers and makes very good meals of them. Once he made omelets for three of us with leftovers of l'Ami Louis's pancake (page 217); it was a fine quick lunch.

12. Desserts

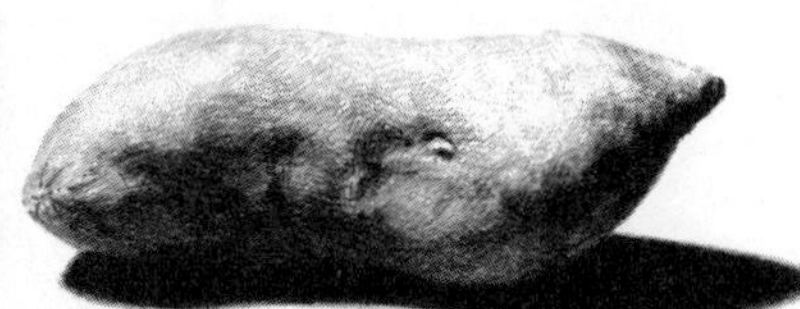

I once taught a potato menu at a cooking school. When the dessert was served, a man walked out before tasting it. He was not going to eat a potato for dessert. I guess real men don't eat potato desserts! In this chapter, the potato plays only a helping hand, and is always mashed.

Frances Brownstone makes the best blintzes I have ever eaten. I added mashed potatoes to her blintz batter for the opportunity to put the recipe in this book. Blintzes are crêpes filled with savory or sweet stuffings.

I make these in a nonstick skillet 5½ inches at the bottom and 8 inches at the top.

Frances's Blintzes

FOR THE BLINTZES:

One ⅓-pound russet potato, cut into 1-inch cubes
3 eggs
½ teaspoon salt
¾ cup flour
1 tablespoon vanilla extract

FOR THE FILLING:

6 ounces (¾ cup) farmer's cheese (see Note) and 3 tablespoons plain yogurt, or 6 ounces cottage cheese
½ cup sugar
1½ tablespoons grated orange peel
2 tablespoons melted butter or margarine
Suzette Syrup (page 226)

In a saucepan, cover the potato slices with cold salted water and bring to a boil. Partially cover and cook for 15 minutes, or until tender.

Drain and mash the potato with a potato masher, ricer, or through a strainer.

Add the eggs and salt to the potatoes. Gradually and alternately add the flour and 1½ cups water. Add 1 tablespoon vanilla extract. Strain the batter, pushing with the back of a spoon to force it through the strainer. Set aside for 1 hour, covered.

Brush the skillet with oil and heat the pan until too hot to touch but not smoking (the batter will clog and not spread if the skillet is too hot). Pour in 3 tablespoons batter and quickly tilt the pan in all directions to spread it evenly in the bottom of the pan. Cook for about 1 minute, gently nudging the sides with a cake turner and shaking the pan to loosen the bottom as the blintz cooks. When the bottom looks golden, flip it over onto a plate. Stack the blintzes on a plate as you make them.

In the food processor or blender, combine the farmer's cheese and yogurt or the cottage cheese, sugar, and grated orange peel; process until smooth.

To fill the blintzes, mound 2 tablespoons of filling in the center of each and roll like a cigarette, then tuck in the ends. If you are not cooking them right away, loosely cover them and set aside.

Just before serving, melt 2 tablespoons butter or margarine in a skillet until it sizzles. Fry the blintzes on all sides for 1 minute. Serve hot with the suzette syrup on the side.

NOTE: If farmer's cheese is unavailable, substitute the same amount of cottage cheese, but in that case do not add yogurt, or the stuffing will be too loose.

Makes sixteen 6-inch blintzes, serving 8

Turos Palascinta

CRÊPES STUFFED WITH COTTAGE CHEESE AND RAISINS

My best friend in college, Henriette Horchler, was Hungarian, and one of my favorite dishes prepared in her home was turos palascinta. I ate lots of turos palascinta in my college years and looked it. I stopped eating desserts when I found a man who told me to lose weight if I wanted to marry him. I did. But I still remember this lovely dessert, and once in a while for special occasions, I splurge.

2 cups cottage cheese
3 tablespoons sour cream
¼ cup sugar
1 cup raisins
16 Frances's Blintzes
Suzette Syrup (recipe follows)

In the bowl of a blender or food processor, combine the cottage cheese, sour cream, and 3 tablespoons of the sugar. Process until creamy. Fold in the raisins.

Fill each crêpe with 2 tablespoons of filling and roll as for the blintzes. Transfer to a 3-quart buttered baking dish. They can be prepared ahead of time; loosely cover and set aside.

Preheat the oven to 325 degrees.

Dribble the suzette syrup over the crêpes, sprinkle with 1 tablespoon sugar, and bake for 10 minutes.

Makes sixteen 6-inch turos palascinta, serving 8

SUZETTE SYRUP

1 1/2 cups freshly squeezed orange juice
1 tablespoon grated orange peel
3 tablespoons unsalted butter
1/4 cup sugar
3 tablespoons Curaçao liquor

In a large skillet, combine the orange juice, orange peel, butter, 1/4 cup sugar, and Curaçao. Bring to a boil and boil down to 1 1/4 cups. Pour over Frances's blintzes or turos palascinta.

Makes 1 1/4 cups syrup

Mini Potato Crêpes with Brown Sugar and Berries

La Mère Blanc was one of the great women cooks of Burgundy in the first half of this century. Her grandson is Georges Blanc, one of the great chefs in France. La Mère Blanc's potato crêpes, excellent as a side dish or an appetizer, also make wonderful dessert crêpes when glazed with brown sugar and served with berries and crème fraîche. (For Passover, substitute 2 tablespoons potato starch for the flour in the batter.) When the berry season is over, I serve the crêpes with brown sugar and sour cream.

3 cups batter from La Mère Blanc's Mini Potato Pancakes (page 6)

FOR GLAZING THE PANCAKES:

Brown sugar
Butter shavings
1 cup sour cream, sweetened with white sugar to taste
1 pint blueberries, raspberries, strawberries, or blackberries sprinkled with 2 tablespoons sugar and 1 tablespoon raspberry liquor

To make the crêpes, follow the directions on page 6.

Place the crêpes on cookie sheets. They can be made several hours before glazing; just cover them with wax paper.

Set the broiler on high.

Sprinkle brown sugar over the crêpes and dot with butter shavings. Glaze for 1 minute under the broiler. Serve immediately with sweetened sour cream and the berries of your choice.

Serves 6 to 8

Bread Pudding

- 6 tablespoons (3/4 stick) butter, softened
- 14 slices Eliza Acton's Potato Bread (page 60)
- 3 1/2 cups milk
- 1 cup heavy cream
- 3 eggs, lightly beaten
- 1/3 cup sugar
- 1 tablespoon vanilla extract
- 1 cup raisins
- Whiskey Custard Sauce (recipe follows)

Preheat the broiler to high. Butter the bread slices on 1 side. Put them on a cookie sheet, buttered side up, and toast under the broiler for 1 minute.

Combine the milk, cream, eggs, sugar, and vanilla and mix well.

Fill a 3-quart round Pyrex baking dish with overlapping layers of bread slices fitting them neatly into the dish and sprinkling each layer with raisins. Pour the milk mixture over, submerging the bread. Cover the bread with aluminum foil and put weights on the bread and set aside for 1 hour.

Preheat oven to 350°F.

Remove the paper and weights and cover the pudding with buttered foil or with a glass lid if you have one for the dish, and bake 1 hour.

Serve warm with a pitcher of whiskey sauce.

Serves 8

Every cook has a favorite bread pudding. Mine is from Janet Cornwall, a fine Canadian cooking teacher. She once cooked bread pudding every day for a week for her hospitalized father. He and his 92-year-old roommate understandably refused to eat hospital food.

WHISKEY CUSTARD SAUCE

8 tablespoons (1 stick) unsalted butter or margarine
1½ cups brown sugar
2 eggs
Pinch salt
⅓ cup Bourbon whiskey

Melt the butter and add the brown sugar. Cook over medium heat until the sugar is dissolved.

Pour the mixture into a blender or a food processor. Add the eggs, salt, and whiskey and blend until smooth and creamy (can be made ahead to this point).

Cook over a low heat until the eggs start to thicken. Serve immediately.

Makes 1½ cups

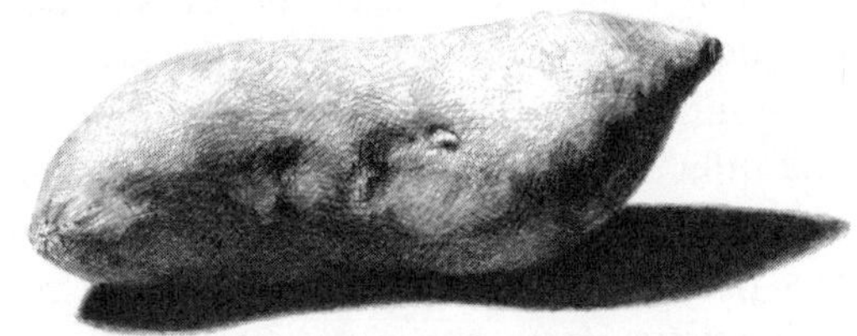

Sweet Potato Soufflé with Whiskey Custard Sauce

1 pound sweet potatoes, peeled and diced into 1-inch cubes (2 cups)
1 tablespoon butter or margarine
1 tablespoon granulated sugar
½ cup heavy cream
¼ cup brown sugar, packed
¼ teaspoon ground cinnamon
⅛ teaspoon grated nutmeg
⅛ teaspoon ground allspice
⅛ teaspoon salt
5 egg whites
Whiskey Custard Sauce (page 228)

In a saucepan, cover the sweet potatoes with a generous amount of cold water. Bring to a boil, partially cover, and cook until tender, about 35 minutes.

Butter a 6-cup mold and sprinkle with sugar. Refrigerate for 30 minutes.

In a saucepan, combine the cream, brown sugar, cinnamon, nutmeg, allspice, and salt. Heat just enough to melt the sugar.

Drain the sweet potatoes. Mash them with a potato masher, ricer or through a strainer. Combine with the cream mixture.

Preheat the oven to 400 degrees.

Beat the egg whites until firm. Fold a quarter of the whites into the sweet potato mixture. Delicately fold the potatoes into the remaining beaten egg whites.

Pour the mixture into the prepared mold and bake for 20 minutes. Serve with whiskey custard sauce.

Serves 6

Sweet Potato Pie

One recipe Sweet Potato Soufflé
One 10-inch partially baked pastry shell made from French Pastry Dough (page 18)
3 tablespoons confectioners' sugar
2 tablespoons ground cinnamon
¼ teaspoon ground allspice
⅛ teaspoon grated nutmeg
½ cup ricotta
½ cup plain yogurt
¼ cup sugar

Preheat the oven to 350 degrees.

Pour the sweet potato soufflé into the partially baked pastry shell and bake for 30 minutes. Cool.

Cut a 10-inch circle out of wax paper and fold it into eighths. Unfold and cut out every other fold, representing pie wedges. Place the 4 remaining pieces of paper on top of the pie. Sprinkle confectioners' sugar on the uncovered wedges of the pie. Shift the paper to cover sugared wedges and sprinkle the spice mixture over the uncovered sections of pie.

Process the ricotta, yogurt, and sugar until smooth and serve with the pie, at room temperature.

Potato Galette Dough

One 1/3-pound russet potato
1 tablespoon active dry yeast
1 tablespoon plus 1 teaspoon sugar
1/2 cup warm milk
1/2 teaspoon salt
2 cups all-purpose flour
4 tablespoons (1/2 stick) unsalted butter, softened
1 egg

In a small saucepan, cover the potato with cold salted water. Bring to a boil, partially cover, and cook for 15 minutes, or until tender. Drain and peel. Mash with a potato masher, ricer, or through a strainer. You should have 1 cup mashed potato, not packed.

Sprinkle the yeast and 1 teaspoon sugar over the warm milk. Set aside for 10 minutes.

Mix the remaining 1 tablespoon sugar and the salt with the flour.

In a heavy-duty mixer or by hand with a wooden spoon, beat together the mashed potatoes, yeast mixture, butter, and egg. Add the flour gradually. Knead until smooth.

Transfer to a large bowl. Cover with a large plastic bag. Let rise until doubled in size. With a wooden spoon, deflate the risen batter, cover with plastic, and refrigerate overnight.

Butter two 11-inch tart or pizza pans. Cut the dough into 2 equal pieces. Roll out the dough to line the bottom of each pan and top with one of the following preparations.

If you are making only 1 galette (1 galette makes 6 large servings), refrigerate and cover the other half of the dough until you need it; it will keep at least 1 week in the refrigerator. (I have never been very successful at freezing yeast dough.)

Enough dough for two 11-inch tart pans with removable bottoms or pizza pans

Galettes are informal country tarts baked with fruits, cream, or nuts, essentially dessert pizzas. I bake them in tart or pizza pans and I always serve a bowl of sweetened sour cream with them.

In the spring and summer, I make galettes with all kinds of berries or fruits; in early fall, with juicy dark plums, and in late autumn and winter, I switch to nuts, whipped cream, and brown sugar.

You can prepare the dough several days ahead of time and keep it covered and refrigerated.

RASPBERRY GALETTE

One 11-inch pan potato galette dough
½ pint raspberries
½ cup sugar plus 1 tablespoon sugar
4 tablespoons (½ stick) butter
¼ cup flour
1 cup sour cream
1 tablespoon framboise liquor

Cover the dough with the raspberries.

Mix ½ cup sugar, butter, and flour into a smooth paste. Sprinkle over the raspberries and set aside for 30 minutes.

Preheat the oven to 400 degrees.

Bake in the center of the oven for 25 minutes. Serve warm with sour cream sweetened with the remaining 1 tablespoon sugar and framboise liqour.

Serves 6

PLUM GALETTE

½ pound dark Italian plums
¼ cup plus 2 tablespoons sugar
1 teaspoon kirsch
8 tablespoons (1 stick) unsalted butter or margarine, softened
One 11-inch pan potato galette dough
Sugar for sprinkling
1 cup sour cream sweetened with 1 tablespoon sugar

Cut the plums in half and pit. Sprinkle them with 2 tablespoons sugar and the kirsch. Set aside for 1 hour.

Mash the butter with the remaining 1/4 cup sugar.

Place the plums, cut sides down, in the soft dough and cover with the sugar and butter mixture. Set aside for 30 minutes.

Preheat the oven to 400 degrees.

Bake 25 minutes in the center of the oven.

To serve, sprinkle sugar over the galette and pass a bowl of sweetened sour cream.

Serves 6

ALMOND GALETTE

1 cup coarsely chopped shelled almonds
One 11-inch tart pan potato galette dough
1/2 cup sugar, plus additional for sprinkling
4 tablespoons (1/2 stick) unsalted butter or margarine, softened
1 cup sour cream sweetened with 1 tablespoon sugar

Sprinkle the almonds over the dough and lightly push them in. Mix the 1/2 cup sugar with the butter or margarine and crumble it over the almonds. Set aside for 30 minutes.

Preheat oven to 400 degrees.

Bake in the middle of the oven for 25 minutes. Sprinkle with sugar and serve with the sweetened sour cream.

Serves 6

BROWN SUGAR AND WHIPPED CREAM GALETTE

One 11-inch pan potato galette dough
1 cup heavy cream
¼ cup brown sugar
About 1 tablespoon butter, in bits
Sugar for sprinkling

Preheat the oven to 350 degrees.

Just before baking the galette, whip the cream until firm. Spread the whipped cream on top of the dough. Sprinkle brown sugar over the surface of the tart and dot with butter.

Bake on the middle shelf of the oven 25 minutes, or until golden brown.

Sprinkle sugar over the galette and eat warm.

Serves 6

Plum Dumplings

- 2/3 pound russet potatoes
- Sugar
- 1 pound Italian plums or cherries, pitted
- 1 egg
- 1 1/2 cups or more flour
- About 1 cup breadcrumbs
- 2 tablespoons butter or margarine, melted
- 1 cup sour cream sweetened with 1 tablespoon sugar

In a saucepan, cover the potatoes with cold salted water. Bring to a boil, partially cover, cook for 30 minutes, or until tender.

Sprinkle sugar over the pitted plums or cherries and set aside for 30 minutes.

Drain and peel the potatoes. Mash them with a potato masher, ricer, or through a strainer.

Bring a large pot of water to a boil to poach the dumplings.

Add the egg and enough flour to the potatoes to make a dough that is firm enough to roll out. It's a little tricky at first because your hands get very sticky, but don't get discouraged, the dough will come together. Gently roll the dough to a 16-inch circle and stamp out 3 1/2-inch circles for the plums or 2-inch circles for the cherries. Reroll the trimmings to make more circles.

Put the plum or cherry in the center of a circle of dough. Lightly brush water around the fruit and enclose it, pressing the dough at the top with your fingers to completely seal the fruit.

Plunge the dumplings into the boiling water and cook for 10 minutes. Drain and quickly dip them in breadcrumbs. The dumplings can be prepared ahead up to this point (keep them for 2 or 3 hours in a baking dish loosely covered with foil).

Reheat in a preheated 300-degree oven with melted butter over them. Sprinkle with sugar and serve immediately with a bowl of sweetened sour cream.

Serves 6

The mashed potatoes in the chocolate keep the cake moist and fresh for several days. It's a perfect cake for large birthday parties.

Chocolate Potato Cake

- 1/3 pound russet potatoes
- 8 ounces bittersweet chocolate or 4 ounces unsweetened chocolate, cut up
- 1 to 1 1/2 cups sugar
- 1/2 pound (2 sticks) unsalted butter
- 4 eggs, separated
- 2 teaspoons vanilla extract
- 2 cups all-purpose flour
- 2 teaspoons double-acting baking powder
- 1/2 teaspoon salt
- 2/3 cup milk
- Chocolate Custard (recipe follows)
- Chocolate Sauce (recipe follows)

For the cake: In a pan, cover the potato(es) with cold salted water and bring to a boil. Partially cover and cook until tender (20 to 25 minutes). Drain, peel, and mash with potato masher, ricer, or through a strainer; you should have 1 cup mashed potatoes, loosely packed.

Melt the cut chocolate in a double boiler.

If you are using bittersweet chocolate, beat 1/2 cup sugar with the butter; if you chose unsweetened chocolate, cream 1 cup sugar with the butter. Beat in the egg yolks, vanilla extract, the melted chocolate, and the mashed potatoes.

Sift the flour, baking powder, and salt together and add to the chocolate mixture alternately with the milk.

Preheat the oven to 350 degrees. Butter two 8-inch layer cake pans.

Bear the egg whites for a minute, then beat in the remaining 1/2 cup sugar. Whip until stiff. Fold gently into the chocolate mixture and pour into the prepared pans.

Bake in the middle of the oven for 35 minutes.

Unmold on a baking rack and cool.

Split each cake in half crosswise, making 4 layers. Spread 2/3 of the chocolate custard on 3 layers, then add the fourth layer cut side up and frost the top and sides of the cake with the remaining chocolate custard. Refrigerate (this will keep for a week in the refrigerator).

One hour before eating the cake, remove from refrigerator. Serve with the chocolate sauce.

Serves 10

CHOCOLATE CUSTARD

1 1/2 tablespoons flour
1 1/2 tablespoons cornstarch
1/3 cup sugar
3 egg yolks
1 cup boiling milk
2 tablespoons butter
3/4 cup heavy cream
3 tablespoons unsweetened cocoa
6 ounces dark bittersweet chocolate, cut into bits

In a 1-quart mixing bowl, combine the sifted flour, cornstarch, and sugar. In a second 1-quart mixing bowl, beat the egg yolks. Pour 1/2 cup of the boiling milk into the flour, mixing vigorously. Combine with the yolks and mix very well.

Reheat the remaining 1/2 cup milk to a boil. Over medium heat, pour the flour/egg mixture into the boiling milk and whisk until it thickens. Remove from heat, add the butter, and whisk until smooth. Cover and set aside.

Meanwhile, boil the heavy cream with the cocoa. Add the chocolate and stir until it becomes a smooth cream.

Whisk the chocolate mixture into the custard, cover with plastic, and refrigerate until very cold before filling and icing the chocolate cake.

CHOCOLATE SAUCE

2/3 cup unsweetened cocoa
3/4 cup sugar
2 tablespoons unsalted butter

In a heavy-bottomed saucepan, combine cocoa, sugar, and 1 cup water. Whisk briskly until the mixture is smooth.

Bring to a boil and simmer for 3 minutes.

Add the butter and bring to a high simmer. Turn off the heat, and pour the sauce into a sauceboat. Serve with the chocolate cake.

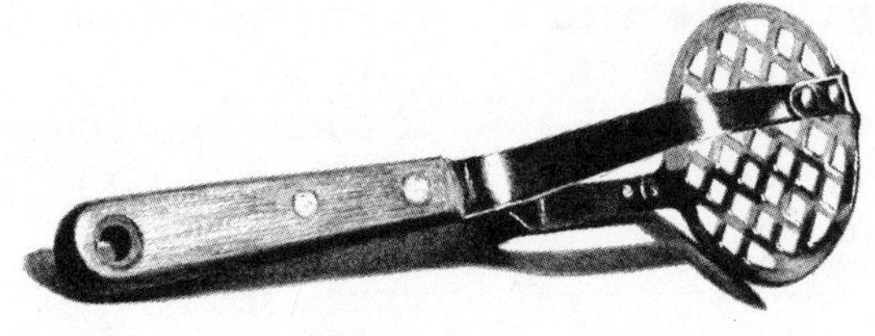

Pound Cake Hilda

This pound cake is a creation of Hilda Fleistein and her sister Erna. Well wrapped, it will keep in the refrigerator for at least 1 month. There's nothing better than a slice of pound cake dipped into a mug of hot tea for a late afternoon break. I have nonstick bundt pans that make unmolding a cinch and also bake the cakes uniformly golden brown.

Two 8-cup bundt pans, buttered

1 pound russet potatoes
1 pound unsalted butter or margarine
7 large eggs, at room temperature
1 pound (2 cups) sugar
1 tablespoon vanilla extract
1 pound (3 1/2 cups) all-purpose flour
1 heaping tablespoon baking powder
1 cup sour cream
2 cups finely ground nuts

In a saucepan, cover the potatoes with a large amount of salted water. Bring to a boil, partially cover, and cook for 30 minutes, or until tender. Drain and peel the potatoes. Mash them with a potato masher, ricer, or through a strainer, 1 potato at a time.

Process the butter in a food processor for 2 or 3 minutes until very smooth and creamy.

In a heavy mixer, at medium speed, beat 1 egg at a time, alternating with small amounts of sugar and butter until all the eggs, sugar, and butter are incorporated in the batter. Add the vanilla extract. Gradually beat in the mashed potatoes.

Sift the flour and baking powder together and, at medium speed, gradually incorporate the flour into the batter. Beat in the sour cream.

Preheat the oven to 350 degrees.

Transfer ½ of the batter to a bowl and fold in the ground nuts.

To fill each pan, put a large spoonful of batter with nuts next to a large spoonful of batter without nuts in 1 layer. For the second layer, alternate the batters to create a checkerboard pattern.

Bake for 1 hour on the middle shelf of the oven. Unmold on a baking rack and cool completely before wrapping and refrigerating. The cake needs at least 1 day to develop its fine flavor.

BIBLIOGRAPHY

BOOKS

Davis, James W., and Stilwell, Nikki Balch. *The Aristocrat in Burlap.* Idaho Potato Commission, 1975.

McGee, Harold. *On Food and Cooking.* New York: Charles Scribner's Sons, 1984.

Root, Waverley. *Food, An Authoritative and Visual History and Dictionary of the Foods of the World.* New York: Simon and Schuster, 1980.

Salaman, Redcliffe. *The History and the Social Influence of the Potato.* Cambridge Paperback Library, 1949.

Weatherford, Jack Mciver. *Indian Givers.* New York: Ballantine Books, 1988.

ARTICLES

Brody, Jane. "The Valuable Potato Goes Global." *The New York Times,* 9 October 1990.

Cook, Jack. "Hot Potatoes." *Organic Gardening,* June 1989.

Scott, Jack Denton. "Praise the Potato." *Reader's Digest* reprint, December 1976.

Steingarten, Jeffrey. "Do the Mash." HG, January 1989.

INDEX

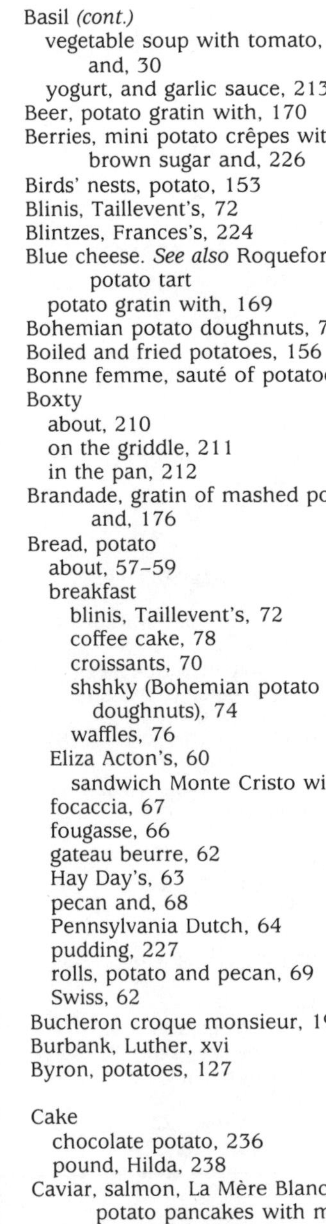

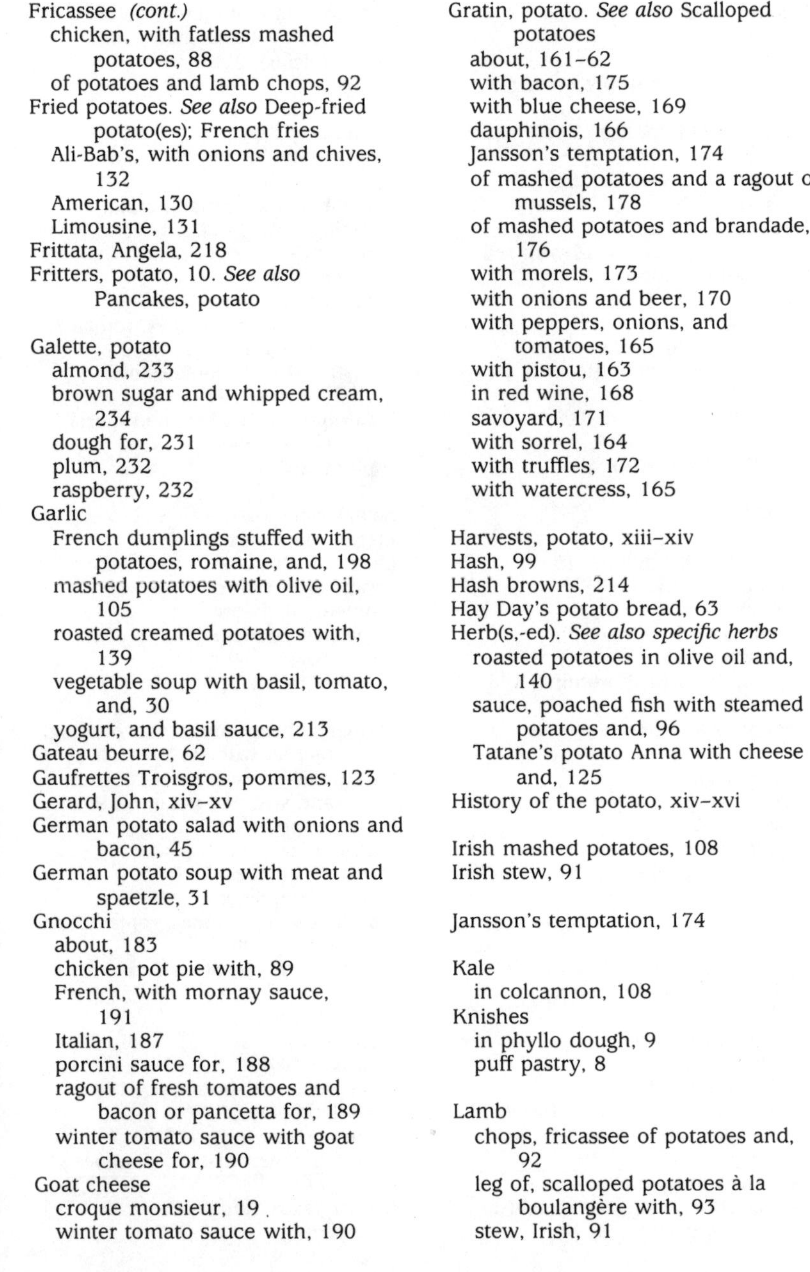

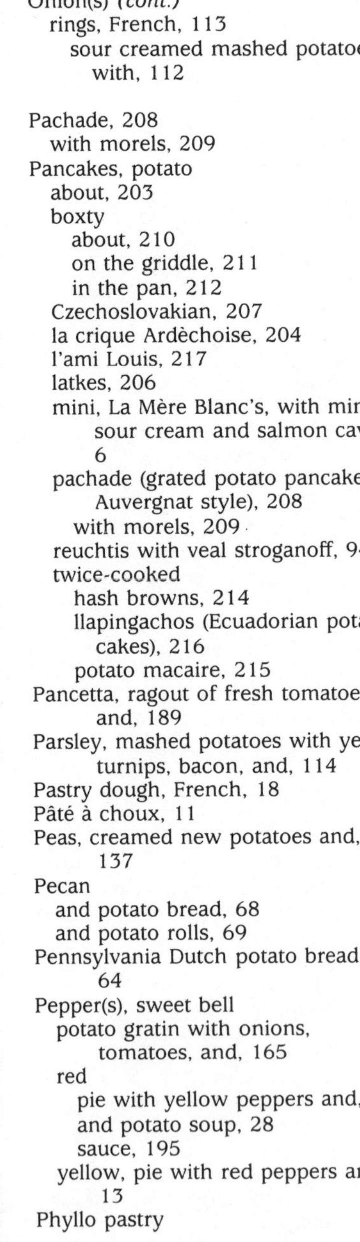

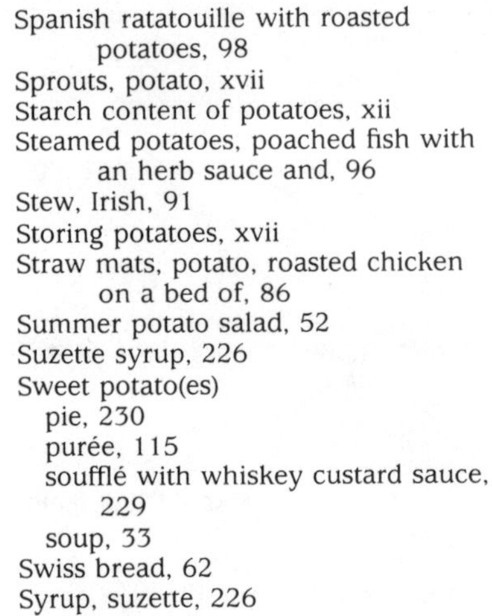